With my compli

Byron C. Hawk

RAWHIDE AND HAYWIRE

PIONEER DAYS IN MONTANA

RAWHIDE
and
HAYWIRE

TRUE TALES OF THE OLD WEST
RECALLED AND ILLUSTRATED
BY SPOKANE'S PAINTER OF WESTERN SCENES

BYRON CLAUDE STORK

 THE WILLIAM-FREDERICK PRESS
NEW YORK   1959

THE WILLIAM-FREDERICK PRESS

391 EAST 149TH STREET   NEW YORK 55, N. Y.

CONTENTS

FOREWORD

BYRON CLAUDE STORK, known as "Spokane's Painter of Western Scenes," was sixty-five when he began putting on canvas the scenes of his early cowboy days in Montana. For years he longed to paint, but he had not time to develop his talent. Herding, or breaking ground for planting, or doing the many laborious tasks the prairie country demanded, if men were to exist there, took all his time.

Without instruction he worked out his own individual painting problems. His art is similar to that of Charley Russell, and quite as fascinating. Many of his paintings have been purchased, and many have been exhibited in the Woman's Club of Spokane, the J.W. Graham's Art Store in Spokane, the Spokane Press Club, at the Washington Art Association in Spokane, the Rainbow Hotel in Great Falls, the Hotel Davenport in Spokane, and elsewhere.

He has also written a book, *Pioneer Days in Montana*, and several magazine articles depicting his hectic life in the wide-open spaces. Recently *True West* published his "Old Buttermilk," a true Western story.

The sincere acclaim of many people and the enjoyment they derive from looking at his paintings of the Old West convince me that his subject matter has an appeal not always created by artists whose talents have been developed by great masters.

The following story tells much, but not all, of Byron Claude Stork's early experiences. And the accompanying photographs of some of his paintings may give an idea what I mean when I say I am proud to be the son of "Spokane's Painter of Western Scenes."

ROBERT P. STORK

INDIANS

I was ten years old in 1888 when I arrived on the Wild Western scene in Montana. Being of the age to enjoy life, I did just that on the last hunting ground of the American Indian. It was a rough, tough life, yet I would not have missed it for anything, and years later I put many of my vivid memories on canvas. I tried to portray the great sprawling plains with their roaming buffalo, antelope, and other denizens of prairie country; I tried to show the strange beauty and haunting loneliness of it all.

I can never forget those immense distances that seemed to swallow up everything, and the sweet aroma of the virgin prairie still remains in my nostrils. It seems to me there has been no era in the world's history when men were more free or made better use of that freedom, despite all tales to the contrary.

Tell me a story of violence or crime of the Old West and I will match it with countless stories about pioneers of real character—brave men, honest men, men and women who spoke through their deeds. Few people today can fully realize the hardships the early settlers had to face in their daily life, hardships accepted as a challegene which had to be met and were met in the bravest fashion. And they did conquer the wilderness and build an empire!

In these days of restrictions, licenses, high taxes, and inflation, it is pleasant to think back to the time when a man could turn his wagon into a peaceful valley unclaimed by anyone and there carve a home in the wilderness (or what appeared to be a wilderness). For there was always life around; God's creatures were everywhere, they would go into hiding when strangers appeared, yet when men proved friendly they would come out and meet his friendship more than halfway.

Yes, it required courage to live in big, undeveloped Montana, but there were many compensations for those who stayed and faced the challenge: free land, lots of room, abundant game, and plenty of fish in the streams—and at times, excitement enough for everyone.

The land was free all right, but not so easy to manage as some might think. It had to be subdued, brought into production. The soil did not plow easy because the turf was often four to six inches deep and very tough. It took *power* to turn it over and we had only small cayuses or oxen.

It takes two seasons in dry areas like Montana and the Dakotas to rot the sod so it can be worked up to produce crops, and in the early days the land had not yet proved what it could grow. But most settlers had as much confidence in its fertility as my father did when he saw the buffalo and the bunch grass waving everywhere like billows on the sea. The grasses were flecked here and there with patches of colorful wild flowers and little splotches of small brush such as snowberry and wild rose, the berries of which made food for countless prairie chickens, snipe, and curlews.

Yes, most of us got along pretty well as long as we behaved, and most of us did; we were too busy generally to do otherwise. But let someone try something shady and he got into trouble up to his neck, and sometimes literally around it. I can remember several occasions when the noose was used to discourage certain undesirable people who had become too antisocial in trying to outwit the other fellow.

Nearly all the settlers were thrifty and resourceful, and the word *resourceful* covered a lot. I wonder how many men today would know how to repair a broken wagon axle with rawhide. How many could use a green sapling, haywire, or rawhide to perform something close to a miracle? I knew a lot of men who had the know-how to do the almost impossible with rawhide and haywire.

We in Montana found many wholesome pleasures to occupy the little spare time we had. We had spelling bees, dances, fake trials, basket socials, and sometimes a preaching- or song-fest, and of course horse racing. Yes, I believe our stalwart Western pioneers of the eighties and nineties compare favorably with pioneers of any time in any place.

I was, as you might say, raised in the lap of the old buffalo hunters, Indian fighters, and trappers. I used to be enchanted by the tales these grizzled old veterans told of the hunt and the fight. I learned many interesting things from them, and many more firsthand and often the hard way.

These old storytellers were in 1888 fresh from the trails, and practically still had the smell of trail dust in their nostrils. Some of them bragged a little but most of them did not have to brag, for the real story was plenty good. If anyone told tall stories people were aware of it and poked fun at them. That's one thing they didn't want, for they had pride, and plenty of it, too.

Occasionally one who prided himself on being an exceptionally good liar would tell some tall tales, but we recognized them for what they were. I remember one fellow who told fantastic tales, but the people knew he was stretching the truth and would laugh at him. But he liked it. I shall call him Jimmie Eastarr.

One day the assessor called at his neat, cozy little ranch in Ming Coules, south of Great Falls, where he had a nice little herd of cattle. Jimmie was always primed and good for a story or two. The assessor dismounted, strode over to where Jimmie was repairing a fence, and said, "I presume you are Mr. Eastarr. You have a nice place here, I will say."

Jimmie replied, "Wal, yes, I am he. But you should see the big place I have up above here if you think this is nice."

The assessor looked over to where the cattle were grazing. "Those sure are fine looking cattle there. Are they yours?"

Jimmie answered, "Oh hell, yes, but you ought to see the others, all thoroughbred Herefords an' lots more than here. An' I have a nice herd of horses up there too, just like the one I rode when I was with Custer before he got killed there on the Little Big Horn. Hey—what you writin' down thar?"

The assessor replied, "I'm only writing down what you said. You see, I'm an assessor."

"Well, I'll be dangblasted for a sidewinder," said Jimmie, as he spat on the grass. "There's one thing more you can write down there, mister, an' that is that Jimmie Eastarr is the biggest damn liar in Cascade County. Jest forget the big herds. Say, dinner should be ready jest now, so put your horse in the barn an' come in; people always eat at Jimmie's house—even the assessor!"

They went in and of course Jimmie told the assessor many more tales. The assessor "forgot" the tales Jimmie had told him and turned in a true listing of Jimmie's holdings.

One thing has always puzzled me, and that is why the government and the Great White Father failed to keep its many promises to the red man. I feel like hanging my head in shame. Lately I am glad to note that some amends have been made, such as honoring the old war chiefs by naming a great power dam in Washington after that great believer in peace, Chief Joseph of the Nez Percés, who avoided war for years but who, when forced to fight, fought as few men can fight. In fact, he really defeated and out-generaled the United States military forces of that time. He made a successful retreat from Oregon to the Bear Paw Mountains in Central Montana, even though burdened by all his squaws and papooses. Undefeated, he finally was induced to surrender under a flag of truce, but the government did not keep the truce then or later.

I shall not attempt to turn historian, because stories about the American Indians are available in all our libraries, but in passing I would emphasize the fact that the incidents leading up to things such as the bloody Custer Massacre are far from inspiring. The Indians were promised homes forever on reservations of their own, but these promises were broken. Then came constant aggression on the part of the white men, the discovery of gold, more broken promises—and war.

I think we should try to get the Indian point of view if we

really want to understand the situation. If they had not fought we would not respect them today. I am quite sure human freedom is worth fighting for, and I think most Americans believe this—and also in fair play. And I believe that if the white man had shown the proper attitude toward the Indian, both races would have benefitted.

Trappers got along with the red men, as did many of the settlers, until prospectors found gold. Men seemed to go crazy with greed after the discovery of gold. It wasn't so much the old prospectors who made the trouble, but strangers who came rushing into the new gold country to take out a fortune in gold!—crazy men, men without honor.

When we first came to Montana in 1888, the Indians were not confined to a reservation. My father Charles F. Stork was in the fifth legislature at Helena when the bill to confine the red man to the reservation first came up in Montana. I remember writing to him and asking him to work against the bill. I see now how wrong I was because the red man would have been better off at that time if put on a reservation instead of trying to fight a hopeless battle with the white man.

During this time there was a Cree Indian camp just west of Great Falls at the mouth of the Sun River. I visited it many times and had several friends among the Indians there. Their sub-chief was called Young-Boy-of-Rocky-Boys-Tribe. Some of them called me Badger Horse because I rode a small pony the color of a badger—a kind of gray with a dark stripe down his back—a good pony in any man's language.

In their camp the Indians gathered in small groups around the tepees. It was interesting to watch them. They talked by using their hands a lot and they grunted and made other strange sounds; a peculiar language, I would say, but very interesting.

The real workers among the Indians were the squaws. They made pemican (berries pounded into tallow), and there were always hides around in various stages of tanning and scraping. These were staked at the edges and pulled tight; then the animal fat was scraped off with bone-handled tools tipped with flint or iron. The braves, when not hunting, which was hard and dangerous work in itself, gathered by themselves and talked of the hunt and of war and horses.

Every place you looked you could see papooses and dogs and more dogs. These Indians really had use for dogs; dog meat was a special company dish. Incidentally, it is said that long before the Indians got horses, which had escaped from the Spaniards, they used dogs to carry burdens. I believe, too, that the Spaniards scalped the Indians before the Indians ever thought of doing such a thing. The Indians then took up the practice in reverse on the white man.

Before the Indians were confined to reservations they became something of a nuisance to the white settlers. They traveled about the country in small groups and often begged food from the settlers. Many a pioneer woman was frightened by them when she was alone, but she always gave them food and was generally unharmed.

There was an old trapper who lived near the mouth of Smith River, usually called Deep Creek. We called him Wolf Jack, although he was mostly after beaver and coyote pelts. His cabin was close to the trail that led off to the south, up in the Tenderfoot Creek country. He was a pretty good-natured fellow with long white locks hanging down upon the shoulders of the leather coat he wore. He claimed he'd been one of Custer's scouts. White men were always welcome in his cabin, but he got tired of visiting Indians.

Once when I went to see him he declared, "I'm goin' to fix those redskins some day; I'm sick an' tired of handin' out grub."

"Jack, you're alone up here," I warned. "You'd better not start anything. The Indians might get you for it."

He answered, "Son, I grew up with those bozos an' I know how to handle 'em. Jes' you wait an' see!"

I didn't wait to see, but I heard later that Jack did know how to handle them. Most old-timeres know the red man is quite spiritual, or I should say superstitious. He fears anybody who acts queer or looks mysterious or different from the average human being. Old Jack knew this and acted accordingly.

One day three big bucks rode up to his cabin, dismounted, and knocked on his door. Jack was prepared for them. He opened his door and the Indians pointed to their mouths and said, "How, How! Eat, eat?" Old Jack said, "Oh sure, come right in!"

The three filed in as Jack put three chairs in a half-circle and fooled around changing them, as if to get them in the right position. He then closed the door tightly and put a chair against it, all the time chuckling to himself and uttering strange things. Finally he got another chair and slammed it down in front of his visitors as if to sit down himself. He then placed an open fifty-pound sack of flour in front of the chairs, all the while performing his incantations.

By this time the Indians were looking uneasy. Jack brought out four large spoons and passed them around, keeping one for himself. Spooning up the dry raw flour and rolling his eyes, he invited them to eat. He pointed to the sack. The large fat Indian buck who seemed to be the leader gave Old Jack a startled look and told his companions, *"Bad medicine!"* With this remark they all tried to get out of the door at once. They made it and hurriedly mounted their horses and raced away, looking back over their shoulders as if they thought the devil himself was after them.

Later on, Old Jack told me many Indians passed up the trail by his cabin, but none of them ever stopped; so I guess the incident turned out to be good medicine for Old Wolf Jack.

The red man had dignity, a dignity all his own. He liked ceremony and could express himself poetically. Old Chief Seattle said, "My words are like the stars and will last forever," meaning, "I am a man of my word." Speaking of some white men, he said, "They speak with a forked tongue." Indians loved bravery and honesty, but unfortunately they found little of either among the white men.

Where did the Indians come from? Perhaps they did not come from anywhere. We might also ask where the buffalo, the wild turkey, and the prairie chicken came from. All are peculiar to this continent. I know I'm sticking my neck out when I point out a few things an anthropologist, an archeologist, or a geologist might not agree with, but I think it takes a lot of loose thinking to connect the Indians with people from outside North America because he is so different from other people in other countries.

The Indians of early North America were strictly of the Stone Age; their tools were made of stone, bone, hide, and sinews. Orientals of that period were workers in bronze and iron, far different from other races. It requires quite a stretch of the imagination to link the language of the Indian with that of people outside America. His customs are certainly his own. A mystery? Yes.

I am willing to accept him as probably the first North American. Where he came from, and when, only God knows. The Indians fitted into their environment. They survived where white men probably could not. I think the Indians were the first Americans; they developed here on this continent, as did the American bison, the prairie chicken, the wild turkey, potatoes, tomatoes, maize, tobacco, etc.

I began to wonder about the red man when my parents brought me to the West. In Montana there were many things still fresh in the minds of the settlers—Custer's last stand on the Little Big Horn, Chief Joseph's war, the Reil Rebellion in Canada, etc. Sitting Bull, Rain in the Face, Crazy Horse, and many others were subjects of daily conversation.

Marks of the tepee rings were still visible on the prairie where the red men laid stones on the edges of the tepees to hold them down when the wind blew, and we could easily make out the tramping grounds of the ponies. I can still trace them in the spring in places where the ground has never been plowed and cropped; there is always a fresh circle greener and of different appearance than the surrounding prairie; in June the grass grows taller, and usually a circle of mushrooms will appear for a week or two after a rain.

INDIANS 17

In the old days elk and antelope horns and bones were generally nearby and also in the prairie country camps. Under a pile of stones on the point of a hill, where there was a good view of the lanscape, could be found graves of people long since forgotten. I also found stone hammers, skinning flints, bone instruments, and grinding stones; all these were a grim reminder that I was, in a sense, a trespasser here.

There remained the old buffalo jumps or slides over which the buffalo were stampeded, falling over cut banks or cliffs to their death so the Indians could acquire subsistence. A dead buffalo meant for the Indians meat, ropes, tepees, and sinews for their bows.

When they got ponies they no longer used the jump to get their bison, but would mount a fast, alert pony, ride up alongside the animal, and either shoot an arrow into him or use a long spear. It required great skill and daring because the bison was large and powerful as well as very fast on his feet, his weight mainly in the front. Talk about turning on a dime, he could do just that; he could pivot and change ends instantly, and those cruel little sharp black horns would come into action, ripping a pony or a man instantly and severely.

A buffalo has many characteristics all his own. For one thing, he has a shaggy thick coat up front to face a storm and not turn his rump to the storm as cattle do. In winter he paws through the deep snow for grass. These things were told me by the old hunters and some I learned myself the hard way.

After the winter of 1886 there were few buffalo left, but I did see a couple of them in 1888, tough old fellows that had survived in the Bad Lands. There are now several herds in the country, herds built up by protective measures. I am glad about this because the buffalo or bison is a real American.

Some of today's roads follow the old buffalo trails. The buffalo would make a trail along the hill for convenience's sake, and often such trails were worn until they were about a foot deep and about that wide too.

The railroad surveys often followed these trails. They also

helped the early trappers and caravans find the mountain passes. It must have been a picturesque sight to see the buffalo ambling along. As these herds numbered in the thousands, sometimes it took days for them to pass. But the white man and his lust for wealth soon spelled their finish.

PIONEER SETTLERS

In 1888, after a long exciting journey in an emigrant car on the new Great Northern Railroad, the Stork family together with their stock, farming equipment, and household goods arrived in the little town of Great Falls, Montana. Besides me were my father and stepmother; my sisters, Ida, fourteen, and Bessie, three; and my brother Charles, ten months old.

You might say we came West about the time of the end of the reign of the red man. (C. M. Russell's *Trails Plowed Under* tells the story of this end very well.) This also was the start of the last great Western land rush. I shall not repeat all the story which I told in my earlier book, *Pioneer Days in Montana*, but I will say it was a grand, rough, tough life for me, a kid of ten. For my dad, however, it was largely hardships and many trials in which the rest of us, of course, shared.

It was my dad's job to establish a new home in the wilds, but before the first year was out my stepmother died, leaving him with a family of kids to look after, the youngest less than a year old. Dad didn't give up; he took up land and built a sod house, he plowed land, and worked for other settlers to keep things going. Fired with determination, he finally succeeded in obtaining 2700 acres of good wheat land eighteen miles south of Great Falls, and the necessary equipment to work them. Shortly after his success with the ranch, he was elected to the fifth legislature from Cascade County.

I remember it was quite a lively session they had. William Jennings Bryan was entering the political arena and mining interests in the state instead of the stockmen were beginning to dominate politics. It is said that bribes were offered and accepted, but I'm glad to say my dad played it straight. Know-

19

ing him as I did, I didn't expect otherwise. Our family had been a family of pioneers for generations; we were always too busy to be bad.

In Great Falls at that time everything had a newness, with changes taking place all around. Growth, hustle and bustle were everywhere. Lewistown and Choteau were new and lively and there were many other stage and cow towns too numerous to mention.

Lewistown was a stockmen's town then but later it became somewhat of a mining town. Fine buildings were being raised every day and it became a trading center for the people from Kendal, Maden, and Whiskey Gulch. Lewistown had good schools and a church or two. It was surrounded by open prairie, fenced here and there by ranchers who wanted a spring or waterhole for their own use.

Cattle, cattle everywhere! They were really slick cattle in the fall. I can still remember those great thick steaks with a nice ring of fat around the edge that we consumed on the roundups. Lewistown had some big stores even then, though this fine little city was 110 miles from the nearest railroad point. Freight teams brought everything into Lewistown. The jerkline outfits were often quite cumbersome, with ten or more horses in each outfit. People traveled by stage from Great Falls or Billings, and in both towns there was a relay system for the horses.

The old stage from Great Falls used to go by the little town of Utica, nestled at the foot of the Little Belt Mountains which were noted for the beautiful sapphires found there. Yogo Creek starts in these mountains on its way to the Judith River. The scenery was beautiful and the game plentiful in the mountains. Tom King, a most interesting old character who was a prospector for gold, lived in these mountains. But more about him later.

Those were the days when settlers were coming in. Here and there could be seen a shack or a cabin by a spring, maybe a furrow plowed in the virgin prairie, and occasionally a fence,

but we could go most any place in any direction without ever
opening a gate. The prairies seemd like a great vacuum that
would never fill up; but once it got started, how it did fill up!
The larger creeks were occupied mainly by large cattle outfits.
There were the Jim Fergus, S. S. Hobson, Russell and Oscar
Steven outfits, besides quite a few others that became well
established early in this part of the country.

I remember well the time night overtook me when I was
near the McDonald ranch. I rode in and asked if I could spend
the night, which wasn't an unusual request in those days. The
boss said, "Sure can, pard, you're welcome as the flowers in
May. We got grub—an' 'nother hand in th' card game will be
okey with me."

The old system was: the stranger was always welcome and
if nobody was home, just cook what you found, but be sure you
washed the dishes when you got through.

The cattlemen didn't take too kindly to settlers coming in,
taking up land, and fencing the range. There were a few warnings such as shootings and burnouts, but the settlers paid little
attention to the warnings. They simply kept coming like a flock
of grasshoppers.

The Fergus County *Argus* carried many of these stories
about the trying times the settlers had in overcoming this
trouble. I've forgotten some of the names now, but I remember
every little while there would be a report of someone myster-
iously shot or a band of sheep stampeded. The situation never
did get out of hand, be it to the honor of Montana, like it did
in Wyoming where events like this almost caused a war in 1889.

All over the West the settlers poured in, some by rail, some
by stagecoach. They arrived by covered wagon in the Judith
River area, for there was no railroad or stagecoach by the river.
They usually arrived in pretty destitute and bedraggled condition, with their wagons needing repairs. It sure took courage
and tenacity for them to start life in a new country.

Among these settlers searching for land of their own were
two families named Briggs and Kurts. They came in by way

of Helena and Great Falls. Along the way they engaged a man Wilbur, who said he knew the trail and could show them good land. He was a bad actor. All he showed them was a watery grave in the Judith River. There were two men, two women, and a little girl in the outfit. Somewhere along the trail Wilbur shot the two men and two women and it was thought he drowned the little girl in a shallow pool of water.

He dumped the bodies in the Judith River at Samples Crossing north of Lewistown, probably figuring they wouldn't be found for some time. He evidently thought he could make good his getaway with their supplies and outfits. Fate stepped in, though; some cowhands crossed the river shortly after the crime was committed and found the bodies. They immediately notified the sheriff's office in Lewistown and Great Falls. A posse was formed and a very nervous Wilbur, still in possession of most of the outfit, was apprehended at Stanford.

The sheriff rushed Wilbur to Great Falls and lodged him in the county jail. People in pioneer days had to behave or they got into trouble up to their neck or literally around it; long drawn-out trials, when there was plenty of evidence of guilt or perhaps a confession, were not the custom in the Old West.

The sheriff and deputy did try to protect their prisoner, for even when a large group of angry citizens stormed the jail demanding that the prisoner be turned over to them, the sheriff refused their request. The sheriff and his deputy had plenty of guts and they faced a mob that knew how to fight and meant business. The mob yelled, "If you don't let us in, we'll get him, even if we have to blow up your jail! So let's get it over with!"

This was no go with the sheriff. The men went off and the sheriff thought he had his prisoner protected. Not for long, though, for the men soon returned and began piling dynamite around the jail.

The sheriff came to the door and said, "Men, I guess you might as well go home. You can save your dynamite. Your man just hung himself. Come in an' see."

Wilbur was hanging by the neck from his bunk. He was

sure dead. Maybe he had help getting that way. Who knows? Or, perhaps, knowing what Western justice was, he decided that ending it himself would be less painful. Men didn't hesitate to punish a crime in 1889 and he knew it.

I'm glad to say we didn't have many such incidents; most people were trustworthy and willing to lend a helping hand to anyone deserving help. Wilbur had been in a lot of trouble, so I would say he was born bad. He was the type vigilantes had to hang at Virginia City to get any semblance of law and order there.

Deputy Hamilton was elected sheriff time after time later on and he proved himself worthy of his office. He was absolutely fearless and usually got his man. No one wanted Joe Hamilton on his trail. Hamilton met an untimely death in 1911 when it is believed he fell into his own trap and was killed by his own men, who mistook him for a kidnapper they were after. The Conrad family which owned the bank in Great Falls was rich. One of the Conrad boys died and soon afterward the body was dug up and carried off, and a demand for ransom was made on the family. A trap was set for the kidnapper between Flouree and Fort Benton. Hamilton's posse was on the trail of the criminal, when it is presumed that one of the men of the posse shot the sheriff by mistake.

Settlers kept coming into Great Falls and the surrounding territory. Great Falls had a big flour mill near Black Eagle Falls, and a brewery was built to make malt and beer out of barley and hops. The Great Falls Meat Company was started and many other business houses sprang up. The cattlemen still predominated and they told the settlers, or "nestors" as some called them, wild tales which made some of them believe they would starve in this new country because wheat would not ripen, hogs all died of mountain fever, and nothing but grass and beef on the hoof would grow here.

One day when I was riding with a cow outfit, we came across a new shack on the prairie north of Belt. An old "sod buster"—as cowmen called farmers—was plowing up that good buffalo and bunch grass. Shorty, my partner, said to me, "We jes' gotta do sumpin', these folks will tear up all the grass an' put us outa job while starvin' themselves in the bargain. I think we oughter hang that old Paris Gibson, he's the feller what's gittin' 'em in these parts."

My dad was raising wheat too so I didn't have much to say. Paris Gibson was one of the founders of Great Falls and, I believe, the first senator from Cascade County. He was quite a promoter and was often called the "Father of Great Falls," but if that old puncher had had his way we would have been short of one senator.

Anyone who has ever seen that beautiful grass waving in the sunshine on the sprawling prairie could not blame the cattlemen for wanting to remain in their profitable business with its wild, free life, but things changed and they had little to say about it, although perhaps they had the right idea. Montana does have dry years and some day all the rich pasture may be gone along with all the grass that can withstand dry spells, the rich grass that cures itself, and is good feed throughout the long winter months.

Perhaps some day when the wind has blown away all the loose soil, we will think back to those early days—days of lush grass and big herds of cattle. Possibly the new dry land system of farming may solve the problem, but we old cowpunchers have our tongues hanging out waiting for the results. We're all getting pretty old and the past doesn't come back; just the memories linger on.

PUNCHING COWS

PRACTICALLY all of Eastern Montana was still cow country in 1888, and each county had its big cow outfits. Many of them had to turn to sheep later on, but at this time if one just mentioned sheep to a cowman he would turn green. It's hard to understand now, but in those days a sheepman was considered a public enemy. A man who started to raise sheep ran the chance of being put out of business. All this was changed later when some cattlemen reluctantly went into the sheep business.

Towns like Choteau, Havre, Saco, Malta, and Landusky were all cowtowns with big outfits. Cattlemen had plenty to eat and it was a wild, free life with big card games and other excitement in the little towns.

A man who could ride and rope could get a job around here any time. Think of it! No license to go fishing or hunting, no tax on land until final proof was made. Uncle Sam sold some tracts for $1.25 an acre. There was plenty of land and cattle, cattle, cattle everywhere!

In my early teens I went to work and soon got so I could ride anything on four feet. I could also rope and I considered myself a first-rate cowhand. Wheat raising seemed too tame for me so I decided I would punch cows and let dad raise wheat. He really did raise wheat, all the old-timers remember, fifty bushels to the acre and shoulder high.

I went to work for the Captain Couch outfit near Cascade and graduated from there to where I considered myself a real cowpuncher and broncotwister, although I must admit I wasn't too good at the business. I got by.

One thing I did seemed to please most of the fellows. I drew pictures of them and their horses, the cattle and camps, etc. Most of the camps I got into got pretty well decorated. But I soon discovered I couldn't live on compliments so I tapered off with this hobby. That is, I did until I saw Charley Russell's pictures in Great Falls at the Silver Dollar and Mint saloons and in the Park Hotel. I could really appreciate the scenes he portrayed so vividly, because I had just come in from the places he had painted. Looking at these canvases, one could almost smell the sweat of the dogies and the dust of the trail. Yes, Charlie sure had it and to me he was the greatest painter of Westerns of them all.

I used to study those pictures and admire Charley's technique, and I guess he was really my teacher without ever knowing it. I got too busy later and decided I couldn't paint anyhow. Then I got married and raised four kids and didn't have time to paint until, when I was sixty-four, I picked it up again. Surprisingly enough, quite a few people seemed to like my paintings, and I sold some of my portrayals of the old Montana scenes that I remembered from my cowpunching days.

I went to work for the Half Circle S Ranch. They had cattle ranging around Cascade, Great Falls, and south of Belt, and clear out to east of Geyser. A widow, Mrs. Sweat, owned the outfit and a fellow by the name of Charley Brewster was the "push" in our camp. He was a nice fellow to work under. We had pretty good luck and everything went fine for quite awhile. I was with a great bunch of punchers, and the cook sure did know how to fix grub.

This good thing and smooth living was too good to last. One cowpuncher put it very bluntly when he said, "Shorty, there's no such thing as a good job. When you got 'er goin' fine, sumpin' always busts." The "bust" in our case was Charley, the boss. He got piled by an old crow bait of a horse and busted his collarbone, so we had to have a new boss. The new boss was a long-limbed man who thought he knew it all, but most of us thought he was mistaken; we didn't have too much confidence in him. We called him Jack to his face, but to his back we called him Beanpole. He was short-tempered and that meant a lot of trouble for us boys. He wasn't too experienced. There's a lot to learn about cows and men and grass and water and brands and cooks. Jack certainly had some good men in the outfit. They knew their work and were loyal and easy to get along with and more than willing to do their work.

One of the first run-ins the new boss had was with our cook, and no boss in his right mind *ever* crosses a roundup cook, unless, of course, he wants to lose him. When the "mulligan mixer" can put out good "chuck" he is master of all he surveys.

When we lost a cook, it was sometimes necessary to go into town to look for one. Usually a small delegation goes in, locates a cook, and then invites him to the best saloon. The drinks are always on the gang and the cook usually wakes up broke and far out on the prairie, with everybody taking a special interest in his welfare.

✦ ✦

We moved our camp beside a little creek which emptied into Belt Creek, as we were rounding up and hazing in all the fat cattle. I pulled in the chuckwagon with old Frenchy, the new cook, inside. Jack told me to put the chuck wagon on a knoll near the creek, only three or four hundred feet from where we were to bed the cattle down for the night.

Frenchy, being pretty range-wise, scowled and said, "Jack, I don't like to cook that close to all those dogies. Isn't there a better place farther away from 'em?" The boss' jaw set, then he spat in the grass, gave the cook a nasty look, and replied firmly, "There's no better place. Shorty, leave the wagon right there, unhitch an' turn the horses into the cavvy."

I did as I was ordered, but I was worried; I could see trouble was coming sure enough. I rode out to work with the other men. It was a beautiful sunny day and all seemed serene. I remember how pretty Old Tiger Butte looked off to the south-west with the purple shade on it, and its white crags and cliffs with a fir tree here and there. All this peace was too good to last, I thought, while we hazed in and cut out until we had about six hundred head of beef cattle.

Nowadays, perhaps, such steers wouldn't be called good beef, but they sold in Chicago in competition with corn-fed cattle and we boys were proud of them. At this time most of the range cattle were a mixed lot. Many were descendants of Mexican dogies; they were long-horned, big with long legs that could travel fast. They could hear all, see all, and smell all. Some were red, some were black, and others had about every kind of spots. It's a long jump from this breed to the modern Durham and the white-faced Hereford cattle of today that are beef clear to the bone and have a docile disposition which makes them easy to handle.

We got the cattle nicely bedded down that evening; when they hit the grass we could hear their long sigh of contentment as they began chewing their cuds, a sure sign that all is well. There was the chance of a few rustlers coming around, old troublemakers who might have to be reckoned with, but all seemed perfect when I left Sad Slim Smith, the night guard, and rode back to camp. The sun was setting, leaving a beautiful painted sky, its colors the kind that only nature knows how to mix. Everything was so peaceful and quiet it made me very happy.

I returned to camp, went to the chuckwagon, and turned my horse loose. Then I sat down on the grass with the other fellows. We ate with our plates on our laps, plates filled with good food and cups filled with coffee that was just right. We were lucky to have Frenchy, a cook who sure knew his stuff. The usual banter went the rounds with first one man then another the butt of some joke.

I told a lively story about Stinky Nevils and his girl over in the Highwood Mountains. When we finally wore that one out, we rolled up in our blankets with our saddles for pillows and dropped off to sleep. As I was dropping off, I heard the boss say one thing I thought made sense: "Boys, keep that cavvy in close." I knew why. Now and then we'd been hearing a rumble of thunder and it would spell work for us if a storm blew up. But this kind of trouble was all in the cowpunching business.

Cowpokes have no trouble eating or sleeping, and so it was with me that night. I was dreaming and snoring in good shape when someone disturbed me. It was the boss pulling my blankets off and ordering, "Shorty, wake up! Get your horse an' get out to the herd quick! Bill, you an' Slim too, it's a bad storm an' it's coming up fast!" We ran to our horses, saddled up, and rode like lightning out to the herd. One of those Montana thunderstorms was coming up all right, and we all knew how rough storms could be out on the open prairie.

The wind came down the coulee in short little gusts at first, then flashes of lightning seemed to be coming nearer by the minute. Suddenly the wind increased in speed and the thunder came louder and more often. We got to the herd and spread out, hoping the storm wouldn't last long. However, we were used to these hard storms, and although each man knew how to handle things in the midst of them, there was always a possibility of disaster.

Abruptly a fierce gust of wind hit us. It blew my slicker up over my head and my horse started to buck like the very Old Nick. I finally got him into the wind, and my slicker eased down to where it belonged. I have often wondered if my horse recognized any of the names I called him in words that would not look well in print, but we boys all used them and our mounts seemed to understand them. I guess it was because they heard them so much.

By this time the steers were milling around pretty badly. Then it happened, and quick! One of those fierce crackling flashes of lightning came as if the very sky had split wide open, then another streak came and still another, followed by a great downpour of rain that pelted down in big drops.

There was the loud bawling of the very scared cattle, their continuous restless movements accompanied by our cuss words; then all at once those cattle broke, poured through and ran past me to wherever their racing feet took them. Except for flashes of lightning and little balls of fire that came from their horns as they collided, it was pitch dark.

My poor horse was crowded here and there and I hoped frantically that he could keep his feet. I knew I'd get considerably mixed up if he didn't. Then, as another flash of lightning came, I made out the hill where our camp was located. The horror of it stunned me: The cattle, six hundred strong, were headed straight for the chuckwagon!

I tried to break through and turn them; it was hopeless, like trying to direct a tornado. I heard swear words, half-French and half-English. Poor old Frenchy, I thought.

I was being carried along relentlessly by pressure from all sides. Then suddenly the cattle separated to avoid a great rock, and thankfully I got up on it. Cattle ran madly past and I clung tightly to the rock and to my horse to keep my balance and place of refuge. And there I stayed until most of the big creatures had raced by.

Then I decided to go back to camp and see how much cook we had left—if any. I was afraid of what I might find. It was certain that Frenchy needed help, and I could not help to round up the cattle until daylight. What I found in camp was a sight to remember. Poor old Frenchy was just getting up out of the mud and trying to get flapjack dough out of his hair and eyes. The place was a mess. Everything was wrecked. Frenchy's prize equipment that he had lovingly taken care of was just about demolished. The chuckwagon was overturned, its tongue broken, its top in tatters. All around us was mud and the still-pelting rain was making it worse.

Fortunately for us all, it was Frenchy's pride in his equipment that was the most hurt. Physically he was whole. But he was moaning, "Damn boss! Beans gone, no cakes for breakfast! Prunes in mud, wagon all smashed! *Sacré mon dieu!*"

Suddenly it began to hail. Frenchy handed me a pail to put over my head and he put a dishpan over his head. We stood there on the lee side of that upside-down chuckwagon while the hailstones hit merrily against the tin and bounced off like ping-pong balls. Some of them were almost the size of such balls too, big enough to cut into my shoulders and hurt. That dishpan and pail sure did service not ordinarily expected of them.

As I stood waiting for the pelting to stop, all at once the comedy of the situation caught me and I laughed uproariously. That really riled Frenchy and he got going. I was sure sorry I didn't understand French, but his ranting sobered me. I was pretty young and I saw humor in a lot of things and situations that other people didn't see.

Much to our relief the hail ceased as abruptly as it had started, and the rumble of thunder went farther and farther to the east. Frenchy and I stayed put because we couldn't straighten things out until daylight.

As the first streak of dawn became visible in the eastern sky I rode off. I could see cattle tracks heading west. I had expected to find them heading east, so I concluded that the men had turned the cattle and headed the wild bunch of fury into the wind to slow them down—a dangerous feat, fine if it works. In this case it seemed it had. For about half an hour I rode on. Finally in the distance I saw one man and a small bunch of quietly grazing cattle. The man proved to be Slim, and he was trying to sew up a hole in his chaps. He was using his knife and a shoestring for his repair job. He had about twenty-five head of cattle with him and, thank God, he wasn't hurt. I was very thankful, for I liked him. The first thing he said to me was, "That was some show las' night, Shorty. Now we gotta git goin'—cattle all over the whole damned country." He was right, for as we rode over the crest of the hill we saw cattle strung out for miles in every direction.

That night the men in our outfit thought Frenchy was made of right good stuff, for in that muddy camp he'd found enough makings to furnish each of us a cup of hot coffee. He also got a new chuckwagon the next day. We boys had all the cattle together by noon of that day too, but we all blamed the new boss for the stampede.

Not long after this our new boss got us into more trouble. Luckily for him he had somebody with him when it happened. Three of us were bringing in a bunch of cattle across Box Elder Creek when Jack led his horse up to what he thought was a good place to water him. Any old-timer would have known what that nice looking place was like. Jack's horse suddenly started to disappear in quicksand.

Pinkie went into quick action. He threw a rope over the horse, snubbed the other end of it to the horn of his saddle, used his spurs—and zowie, out came the dripping wet, scared animal. Wise-guy Jack was still stuck and he was going down fast with that gurgling sound sand makes when it sucks things to destruction. You can't throw a rope over a man's neck like over a horse's, expecting to yank him free. Luckily, Pinkie was a fast thinker; he flung his rope over a small dead cottonwood tree and yanked it down; then he threw it close to Jack and commanded him to put it under his arms. Then he told us all to pull. Out came Jack, clinging desperately to the log. His face was dead-white under his leathery skin. He was sure getting educated fast and for free in the hard old-fashioned way, in the way that always sticks.

The next day we miraculously got a new boss, by the name of Wild Bill Hannigan. He was from Big Sandy and was supposed to know cattle; at least all us cowhands hoped he did for we sure didn't want to get fooled again on a boss. We all knew about the real punchers down Big Sandy way, and so we just kept our fingers crossed, hoping all the time for the best. We wondered why he was called Wild Bill, but we did our wondering silently.

Wild Bill had a good rig and he stepped lively on his springy feet, his legs crooked as if he'd lived in the saddle mostly on broncs. So Slim McCarthy said, "That boy is the real cheese if I knows what!"

Our new boss and the boys moved camp to Otter Creek

Bench near Kirby where there was lots of grass and good water. Cowboy heaven, I called it, as there was plenty of sunshine and first-rate bedding ground too.

Pinkie brought in two fat antelope, so it was antelope steak for all. An antelope is about the finest eating there is. They are also the fastest things on feet, running gracefully and easily, beautiful little fellows, weighing about a hundred pounds. Their eyes are large and bulging and they seem to see everything in a blink of an eyelash. But they are curious little fellows. If they see you disappear suddenly, for example if you lie down in the grass, they're apt to be curious enough to come circling back to see how come; and of course that's their mistake, poor creatures.

The picturesque grassy slopes on the foothills south of Kirby, Geyser, Belt, and Stanford used to have a regular trail where antelope would scout around the edge of the hills unmolested.

One sunny day we moved camp to a nice spring and camped on the bench south of Geyser. We didn't get many Half Circle S cattle here, but this was Association stuff, so I learned about quite a few new brands. We were getting closer to the town of Geyser. It had a small saloon, a store, and a hotel, and was what you might call a typical stage town. Pat O'Hara had a ranch in this locale; some of the old-timers called him Pat Geyser, because he owned everything in the town, but he had a lot of friends and he ran a square poker game.

The boss, thinking he'd pull a fast one, tried to keep us out of Geyser on payday night. He told Old Frenchy to serve supper late on payday. But this didn't always make the boys stay in camp, especially the cowboys who were well fed and rarin' to go.

I learned my lesson very well when I was younger: don't play poker to make money! I learned you always lose your money and a lot of sleep. If you must gamble, buy out the gambling joint and get on the other side of the table; otherwise stay out. That's for me.

One payday morning when we were riding out, admiring the scenery after having our breakfast, I noticed Slim wasn't any too chipper. He answered questions with a short "no" or "yes," and he looked moody so I just rode along enjoying nature's scenery and left him alone. I thought he'd come out of it, and he did, but it kind of surprised me when he said, "Shorty, why are cooks such dictators? Frenchy is just a plain dictator, an' he can't cook. Betcha I could beat him at it. Now last year on the Shankin roundup we had an old cook named Swede Olson an' he could really cook! He knew how to handle food. His flapjacks were so light an' fluffy I had to stick my fork into 'em to keep 'em from floatin' off." He gazed moodily into the distance while feeling for his purse—or the place where it rested for short spells.

I thought it was my duty to straighten him out, so I said, "See here, Slim, you know Frenchy is a pretty good ol' mulligan mixer, an' he sure is agreeable, which is more than you can say for some cooks. Besides, everybody knows French cooks are the best kind. They're the only kind that put out feed like they got in that big camp back in New York City, the one they call the Waldorf-Astoria. I jus' think you've got too much money, or you've lost your hankerin' for good grub."

Slim answered me: "Well, Shorty, I still say Frenchy's a dictator like most cooks. Why he even tells old Wild Bill where an' when to camp. He gets away with it too. An' another thing, supper is too damn late on payday. Moonlight an' beans, bah! I want to go into Geyser an' get me four aces an' see the boys. Besides, Pinkie told me he saw Pat O'Hara get in six cases of Old Crow whisky. I want to get a bottle for my cough; it's good for pain in the chest too, they say. I tell you, no dictator tells Slim what to do or where to head! Anyhow, I aim to see my old pardner Sweetwater Bill down there at Pat's place. . . ."

Next morning, as the sun was rising and the chuck was sizzling in the pan, Slim and I sat feeding our faces and saying nothing. Thinking I'd break the monotony, I said, "How 'bout it, Slim, did you get those four aces last night over in Geyser?"

Slim straightened up a little and swallowed hard as if a lump in his throat bothered him. Then he replied, "Some folks got no business to 'tend to, so they jus' look after other peoples'. Don't you suppose I'd notify you if I did get 'em four aces? I'll tell you this, though, Pat O'Hara is sure nice. Nobody 'preciates the interest he takes in us boys. He even give me this as a token of friendship when I lit out for camp this mornin'." He patted a bulge in his hip pocket that looked like a bottle.

After grub was taken care of, the boss, who was scattering the riders, came up to me and said, "Shorty, you an' Slim take in Arrow Creek an' Square Butte. See what you can find. Slim, just leave that bottle here in camp. We might need it if some of those big rattlers get too friendly." Slim grudgingly handed the bottle over to the boss and we were on our way for another day on the range.

We gave our mounts their usual morning workout to get them started in the right direction on a cool morning, and then headed out to the range and the trail leading to Old Square Butte. In the distance we could see the butte with its shadows growing shorter and shorter as the sun rose higher in the sky, taking the dew off the sage and grass.

Slim suddenly remarked, "You know, Shorty, I liked that feed Frenchy put out this mornin'; guess he's a pretty good cook at that, an' he's right pleasant this mornin', too. Maybe he's no dictator at all. Anyhow, cow camps don't have dictators, and if they do they don't last long; guess maybe Frenchy changed or somethin'."

I replied, "Slim, I'll bet you're stone-broke an' kinda lovin' everybody, an' that's the way I like to see you."

The horse Slim was riding, Old Baldy, was a veteran of many a roundup, and he shook his head knowingly, as if to say, "This is old stuff to me." We trotted off, stirring up little puffs of dust as we went through the grass and sagebrush on the trail leading to the range near Square Butte, east of the Highwood Mountains where the meadow larks always sing by the creeks at roundup time.

We had a tough time that day. Several new riders came to join us, among them Angus McDonald and an Americanized Englishman we called Smitty, his name being Smith. He could sure ride in spite of the fact that he spoke what we called the King's English, except when a few cuss words were called for. McDonald we nicknamed Mack; he chewed snuff and didn't like whisky. Truly a strange Scotsman. Some of the boys heard he was a remittance man, which means he probably got into trouble at home in Scotland and his pa sent him away with an allowance. We didn't ask any questions in a camp outfit. If a man was square with the bunch and could do his job, all went well. Mack had been fair and the boys liked him.

We wrangled a big bunch that day and I was tired, ready to roll up in the old blanket. But there was a little confusion going on. Pinkie had hurt his foot when his horse slipped and fell on it, doubling it back. It was quite painful. Frenchie put on a hot pack to give Pinkie some relief. Pinkie was plenty tough, so I knew he would be back in the saddle again in a day or so.

The kid Davis (he was our black sheep) pulled a bad one on Smitty, but I guess the kid didn't know any better; he was pretty young—only sixteen—and new on the range. He thought all new punchers should be initiated like they do in high school. We had an open camp and slept on the ground. We had to watch for rattlesnakes so most of us shook out our blankets before we rolled up for forty winks, which was all we got sometimes. The kid curled up a bull whip that first night Smitty was with us and put it into Smitty's bed. Smitty nearly passed out when he found that cold, slick thing curled up in his bed. We all would have done the same thing. Smitty just froze in his tracks, or maybe I should say bed, and then started to yell, "For God's sake, do something! I'm sitting on a rattler! If I move and let him up he'll fix me for sure! Fellows, quick! Look under me and see; can you kill him before he kills me?"

This outburst started things fast. Tex Sancho grabbed his
.45 and pulled the covers back very gently till he saw the black
thing coiled up. Then he grabbed and pulled it out gingerly
and said something that sounded like *"diablo!"* I guess he
wanted to laugh, but he knew that would be dangerous. He
just walked away from where Smitty was still sitting. Smitty
was shaking and pale as a ghost until Slim passed him a jolt
from the bottle Pat O'Hara had given him the night before.
Then he came to with a bang. He looked the bunch over coldly
and said, "If this is the way you hombres treat a new hand in
this outfit, this is for all of you." He spat on the ground twice,
looking us all in the face. Then he said, as if by afterthought,
"I can lick any damn son of a bitch that did this damn yellow
trick!" He reached under his blanket and brought out a shiny
.45 Colt, saying, "Now, don't hurry, boys, but who's first? This
thing hurts when it goes off!"

Confidentially, I don't think he could have hit an elephant
the way he was shaking, but we all were more than a little
frightened, and more than a little ashamed, since we knew he
had reason to be riled up.

Tex Sancho stepped up close and said, "Now Smitty, hold
your fire. Let's see who done this before you start shootin'. Now,
fellows, who's been in camp today?"

Slim answered very solemnly, "Only Frenchy, of course, an'
he wouldn't do no such trashy trick."

I spoke up then, "You know the kid was here in camp
peelin' potatoes for Frenchy. I think he's out there right now
with Frenchy."

They told me to go and bring the kid in. Tex said, "Get
him, Shorty, we've got to have a trial."

I went out to the chuck wagon and told Davis the boys
wanted to see him out by the bedding ground right away. He
tried to play it slick and stall, but I told him they wanted him
right now and he better not waste any time getting over there.
The poor fool kid turned pale, but he had to learn that we
didn't play that way in this outfit. Sure I felt sorry for him, but

he had to learn his lesson and the quicker he learned the better off he would be in later life.

He followed me slowly and said, "Do I have to go now? What do they want with me?"

I looked at him closely. "Kid, I think you know what they want, an' you'd better 'fess up so no innocent person will get hurt."

This had a frightening effect on him because he said, "Oh, Shorty, will they hang me? Will they?"

I thought I'd really scare him and maybe cure him of pulling such kiddish capers, so I told him, "I know they got a rope ready, but tell 'em like a man an' take your medicine."

All he said as he swallowed a big lump in his throat was, "Let's go, Shorty." He walked right up to Smitty when we reached the grounds and said, "Well, I did it. I'm sorry. Really I didn't mean for anybody to get hurt."

The poor kid kept putting his fingers to his neck and swallowing as if that big lump was still bothering him. Sancho figured what the kid was thinking because he said, "We ain't hangin' no kids around here. You better pack up your belongings an' get ready to go home tomorrow."

The kid broke down and cried like a baby; I think this hurt his feelings almost as bad as a rope around his neck would have hurt his neck. He hung his head in shame, went over to his blankets and curled up as if he was going to sleep, but I'm sure he didn't get too much sleep that night.

The next morning was beautiful, with the sun shining brightly and the meadow larks singing. The boss brought the kid his check while we were eating. He left our outfit without even finishing the good chuck Frenchy had prepared for us the last day in this camping spot. Yes, we were all for leaving this camp site, but not by request like the poor kid was doing. We all wished him luck and Godspeed. He sure looked like he had lost the only friend he ever had as he walked away from where we were all sitting and eating. . . .

We moved camp a little farther up in the hills.

Let me tell you about a few of the wranglers I became acquainted with in my days on the range in this outfit. There was Slim McCarthy, from whom I learned a lot about dogies, ranges, brands, and horses. Whenever he got something on one of the boys he would razz them, especially if he got something funny on them. Regardless of this, the boys liked Slim. He was a dandy fellow until he got a few drinks under his belt; then he thought he was a gambler. But we didn't have time to play cards or drink in camp, for this was a business that required a keen mind and an active body. And Old Bill, the boss, didn't stand for any foolishness while the cowhands were on the job. I sure liked Slim, and the boss too.

Old Bill was a different person when he got to where the bright lights shine. One time in Belt he tried to ride three horses all at once and standing, changing from one to the other. He was doing fairly well until a dog fight in the street frightened the horses. Hell broke loose and the show was over as far as Bill was concerned.

Sancho we called Tex, though he was a Mexican. Some of the boys called him a greaser, but not to his face, of course; I can tell you that for sure. Sancho came all the way from Mexico to Montana with the Teddy Blue Abbott and the Granville Stewart outfits and worked for a lot of big outfits in the Judith Basin area. He told us stories about wrangling horses for the N-Bar Ranch, the Oscar Stevens Ranch, and the D.H.S. outfits. He also talked and acted as if he had a señorita down Mexico way. He sang songs about Mexico in a manner that even had the cattle acting blissful. Sancho could ride and rope and knew practically all the brands.

Slim said that Sancho, whether a greaser or not, could camp on his doorstep any time. I sure liked Sancho's riggin's. He was the proud possessor of a very beautiful Mexican saddle heavy with decorations.

The horn was low and the bridle had a silver guard on each side. He had chaps that were the envy of every one of the boys—two tones of real leather and could turn the sharpest thorn there was in Montana (and, believe me, some of them are plenty sharp). Sancho threw a long rope that was a showpiece too. He was mighty proud of his rope, which was a mixture of hemp fiber and horsehair. When he let go with that rope he always got something, and it wasn't just atmosphere either.

Pinkie, a typical cowhand, so nicknamed because of his light hair and rosy cheeks, was anything but the sissy his name might indicate. He was all cowboy from the top of his fair head to the toes of his cowboy boots.

Slippery Bill Conner was another of our experienced cowhands. Work was his middle name. He liked to gamble, too, and was slippery as far as the game was concerned, but he usually lost. Losing didn't bother him because he liked the game.

Eagle Eye got his name because looking things over was his long suit. This sure helped on the range where there is no limit to distance and you had to be able to recognize brands a long way off.

Hay Head Brown was an odd sort of fellow to find in a cowpunching outfit. He liked to read Bible stories. He was an all-around cowboy, though, a good rider and roper; but he was a lot like the rest of us when he got angry. Then he would turn loose with as many curse words as any of us.

Old Bronco Pete liked to night herd the horses and spout big stories, and he was good at both. He could usually be depended on to have the cavvy on hand at the right time. When we needed horses it was important to have someone like Pete in camp.

Bronco Pete and the bear were almost the Waterloo for both Sancho and me. Pete and I were talking one night. Pete suddenly said, "Them broncs were sure uneasy last night, snortin' and runnin' like crazy, actin' the same way that night over in Belt when that stinker had those three queens and I was bluffin' with a pair of deuces and won the pot. Shorty, you think there might be a bear up in that coulee that runs toward Loggin' Creek?"

I sat and thought for a few moments. "It could be, for horses sure don't like bears around. Tell you what I'll do, I'll get Sancho to go out with us as soon as it gets dark. [Bears are always bigger after dark.] Maybe we can rope the bear an' get some meat." [It's the hope of every cowboy to rope a bear at some time in his wrangling and cowpunching career.]

I talked over the situation with Sancho, and we decided to go out into the coulee. So off we went after it got real dark. We watched and waited. The dew was kind of damp and it got real cold. The wind came down that coulee sighing like a monster in chains. Suddenly the wind stopped blowing and my breath sounded like Old Man Sander's sawmill in action. We just crouched and waited for the bear. It was now very quiet, but once in a while I heard some frightening noise coming from the vicinity of Tiger Butte. A coyote howled or an owl got a prairie chicken or something, judging from the commotion we heard in the bushes.

The pale moon was just showing a little streak of light over the hill to the south, when I thought I heard a noise. It was a faint sound and I listened with both ears cocked for the possibility that it might be the bear, but I heard nothing more. In fact, it got so quiet it seemed more like a Quaker prayer meeting. I thought how nice it would be to be able to hit the hay, or I should say saddle, since that is what we used for pillows. Maybe we were a couple of chumps to come out here and miss all the good sleep we could be enjoying after a hard day. Time passed slowly with no one to talk to and I was really getting awfully tired. Still, I was diligently watching over the hill when suddenly, yes, I saw a shadow move on the trail over where the thorn apple bushes stood.

Instantly I thought to warn Sancho of the danger lurking so near both of us—the quail whistle that would not tell the bear of my whereabouts—so I gave the quail call, and was immediately answered by the reply call from Sancho. I watched intently, wishing I had Eagle Eyes' ability to see things. Finally I spotted the bear. He was lingering under the cover of the hill, suspicious of danger lurking nearby. But he must have decided he would take care of whatever might be in the darkness, because he slowly ambled down the trail by the big rock where Sancho was hiding.

Swish! I heard that peculiar sound of Sancho's rope; that heavy rope made a sound different from any other rope. I heard a thud and grunts, and then a growl rent the air. I saw a black woolly ball go end over end. Mr. Bear seemed kind of addled but he got up and gave with a run, and that heavy rope zinged like a busted banjo string. I prayed the rope would hold. Sancho had the rope snubbed to a point of rock, and the rock seemed plenty secure, but that bear didn't give up. He fought the rope like a mad hyena. He kept pawing and rolling around trying to free himself. He tried to bite the rope, but to no avail.

I looked away from the bear and saw Sancho's horse had tried to stampede through a bunch of aspens and had got stuck fast. He couldn't budge and was trembling like a leaf in a strong wind. We had plenty to do with the bear, so we couldn't help the poor horse right then.

Sancho called, "Shorty, if I could get this rope over the rock a litle tighter, I could snub him up an' hogtie him. We can't shoot out here so close to the cavvy or we'll stampede all the horses."

Here was my chance, I thought, to show how brave I could be despite my size. I was plenty scared. I felt like a wet rat and was trembling about as bad as Sancho's horse, but I went on, slipped slowly over to the rock and lifted the rope over. Oh boy! it seemed I could count the teeth the bear was showing with each snarl and, believe me, I wasn't anxious to get any closer than the situation demanded. Sancho quickly tightened the rope as I got over the rock. Then things *really* started happening. The bear chewed and clawed at the rope. He was clawing like hell all around where he was being held captive when suddenly I heard something snap and Sancho yelled, "Run, Shorty, run! He's comin'!"

I didn't look around or anything, you can bet. I did run, and like I never had before. I guess Sancho ran too, but in what direction I never knew, because I could hear that bear coming right at me. He was really coming fast, too, considering how big he was. I could feel his warm breath on my neck and that sure gave me the chills, even if his breath was hot on my neck. I thought of my Maker and of all the bad things I had done and never taken time to ask forgiveness for. Something like that makes a person wish he had lived a better life, let me tell you!

Suddenly I fell into a washout in the coulee the rains had made. I felt that God had answered my prayers for a hole to crawl into and, believe it or not, that bear went right over me and kept right on running. I'll bet he was going twenty miles an hour. I looked up and saw about eight feet of Sancho's rope still tied around his neck. Needless to say, I cared nothing about the rope, but I thought for a minute that Sancho was going to go after his precious rope when he got to where I was still crouched in the hole.

The first thing Sancho said was, "Shorty, he's got part of my rope!"

I looked at him helplessly. "You're not going to worry about that rope when you just escaped with your life, are you?"

Next morning when we told the boys of our escapade with the bear they said we were dreamers, and of course we couldn't prove our tale except to show them that part of Sancho's rope was missing. Tales like this are often told in a cow camp, and after this we were always called the "bear hunters." They laughed like fools every time they thought of our escape from our "bear."

It isn't all fun in a cow camp. We had a rough day following the night of the bear hunt. We had to haze in all the fat cattle. The crags and buttes of the mountain country are sure rough. We had to cut all the fat cattle out of the herd in preparation for shipment, besides trying to hold them together. If there were any young stock in the bunch, they had to be branded. The young stock over six months old are called mavericks and can be branded by the cowpuncher who finds them, if they are not following their mama. We put the brand of the mother on the calf, although once in a while a young calf had a different brand than that carried by the mother. Usually the mavericks are only small stuff, six months or sometimes even younger.

We had to take turns on night guard, and it really gets lonely out there under the stars. I liked it, though; it gave me a feeling of how wonderful God made this universe for all mankind and also for the animal kingdom. The stars shine and wink at a person like diamonds in the sky.

We sang to the dogies while on guard duty, such songs as "Last Night as I Lay on the Prairie." The cows seemed to be more contented after we sang to them because during the singing the cattle can't hear the strange noises on the range that might cause a stampede.

THE HOMESTEAD

OUR OUTFIT at Geyser was about through, and I wanted to
see the Judith Basin, so I went on to Stanford, about sixty-five
miles southeast of Great Falls. Stanford was only a little cluster
of cabins, two saloons, a post office, and a big store owned by
Stow and Mitchell. Sheepmen were coming into Stanford. The
Sage Creek Sheep Company and Bowers Brothers were two of
the big outfits. But I didn't like sheep and I didn't want to have
to apologize to any of the cowpunchers for working for a
sheepman.

I went back to Great Falls and took up a homestead near
Tiger Butte. The law made it necessary to live on such land
six months of the year for from five to eight years and also
make certain improvements on the land. I bought a grubstake
and put up a shack. French Louie Archambault, an honest old-
timer, gave me an old cook stove, but I had to put tin cans
under it for legs; it didn't have much of anything except a
pretty good firebox to cook over. I had things plenty tough
that first winter. I had to sleep on the floor close to the stove
so I could keep fairly warm on those cold winter nights that
are so common in Montana.

After filing the papers for my claim, buying lumber to build
my shack, paying for getting it hauled out to my land, and
buying a few staples in the line of groceries, I was almost
broke. I went to work for Mr. Betts, a neighbor, so I could buy
enough more groceries to see me through the long, cold winter.
It was forty miles to Great Falls, and the snow got plenty deep
in the winter. It was important to have a few commodities on
hand as well as a grubstake in this kind of weather in this part
of the country.

45

I got along nicely at the Betts place. Their son Darrow and I got along well together: we were about the same age. We did the ranch work and rode for cattle.

Mr. Betts was a staunch Republican. An election was coming up and it was my first year to vote, since I had just turned twenty-one. The Democratic candidate that year was William Jennings Bryan, and I thought he was *the man*. Like lots of other young men, I thought I knew more than anybody else. Mr. Betts thought it his duty to educate me in the political picture. Of course I didn't appreciate his education much then, but as I look back now I can understand his interest in trying to give me the facts.

The family left Mr. Betts and me alone to argue out our differences of opinion. They never took sides. Needless to say, my candidate lost; even though I had made my own decision, I voted for the wrong man.

Ranch work on the Betts ranch was over shortly after the election. Now young Darrow could take over the work without any outside help. I went back to my homestead on Tiger Butte and played solitaire by the hour just to pass the time. Once in a while I hunted jack rabbits and visited my neighbors when the weather permitted. I didn't have a very fertile piece of land but I kept my 160 acres and bought forty more. Back in those days you could buy certain tracts of land for $1.25 an acre.

This last piece of land gave me a dandy spring that came out of a cleft in a rock, fell straight down about two feet, and then cascaded off into a nice creek. My spring was surrounded by an acre of willows that was often the feeding place for prairie chickens. Sometimes I could hear them light on the comb of the roof of my shack, especially if I slept late. Once in a while I would steal, softly to the door, open it slowly, and bag myself a couple of these tasty bits of wild game. I always felt guilty about shooting them; I was more or less a humanitarian at heart and hated to shoot any little creature. But one has to eat on the prairie, I told myself.

These prairie chickens were the easiest wild game to shoot,

for they do not fly zigzag like the grouse does. Prairie chicken fly straight and sail off straight—an easy target for anyone with a gun. They are practically extinct today because of that factor.

It was beautiful and wild up on my homestead. The hills were big, the coulees deep, and the scenery beautiful. Old Tiger Butte watched over all this beauty like a guardian angel. Looking over the wide expanse I often wondered how many secrets Old Tiger Butte held, towering up there in the clouds and looking down on the hills, the trees, and mountain streams as well as on all the people who had passed by it in their travels.

I became acquainted with a number of people in the wide area around my homestead. There was a prospector, Old Man Temple, who used to come out of Dry Fork with a pack mule loaded with high grade ore. Nobody could find out where he got the ore. Some said it was just the stuff prospectors and mining men call "float," a mineral lead that has blown up.

Nice girls were few and a long way apart. There were about twenty-five miles between them out on the prairie, and there was a lot of competition for their hands or to escort them to the dances held in a hall on Upper Sand Coulee Creek near Evans' post office.

A neighbor boy once invited me to a dance at his home. But he had invited the girl I was planning on escorting to the next dance. I had been working for the girl's father for a few days when the invitation was extended, and I accepted with the intention of taking my boss' daughter. When I found out later what the boy had done behind my back, I figured it was time to get the old head working and think out something to get even with him, and also keep him from taking my girl to the dance. Her name was Mable and she lived about forty miles from Great Falls. Knowing she wanted a new dress for the dance, I suggested to her father in her presence, "Mr. Watrous, I have some business I'd like to transact in town; if you don't mind, I think I'll go into town tomorrow." Mr. Watrous was agreeable, and asked me to take in a load of baled hay. I quickly agreed and looked over to where Mable was standing. She said,

"Pa, I can go in with Shorty and get my new dress." I was hoping she would suggest riding in with me since I had no intention of getting back in time for the dance.

Mable and I went into Great Falls the next morning, quite early since it was a long way to go. Mable bought herself a new dress. Needless to say, I did not get my business taken care of that day and we decided to stay overnight. Mable missed the dance at Fred's place, but she sure enjoyed herself at the dance to which I took her in Great Falls.

This little prank I pulled on Fred brings to mind another time two of us boys put it over on a fellow who came to call on a nice young girl we were both quite fond of. She did not seem to have much time for either of us, but that did not dampen our feelings toward her. The other boy and I concocted a scheme to make her caller look ridiculous and get ourselves in the running with her—or so we thought. When he came to call on her and tied his horse to the hitching post, we placed a piece of curled barbed wire under the saddle and set it carefully back in place. We waited for what seemed a long time before the fellow came out of the house with the girl, who sent him off with some endearing words. I still don't know if she really cared for him or not, but these parting words made us all the more impatient for him to get onto the horse. Believe me, things sure did happen! The horse put his head down, his tail came up, and the next we saw of the boy he was up in the air looking as if he wanted to fly. But nothing like that happened, and he came down and hit the ground hard and lay there motionless.

The horse had broke loose. That piece of barbed wire had fallen out in the horse's frantic struggle to free itself of the prickly thing. My partner and I rushed up, to show the girl we were manly enough to offer our services to her fallen suitor, but the young lady indignantly waved us aside and took care of the poor fellow herself, in such a way that I enviously wished I had been the one to get hurt. She sure gave him loving care. My pal gave me a funny look and we sneaked away feeling pretty chagrined.

✓ ✓

A new family moved into the Red Butte district which is now called Eden; the Scotts had two daughters and, believe me, they had plenty of suitors from far and wide. My affection turned toward daughter Olive, and she seemed to return my feelings until an older man made her acquaintance. He was richer than me. My friend Ted and I decided we should do something about the situation; we felt he was poaching in our territory. The man lived quite a distance away and we felt he didn't belong in our area competing for the love of the few girls that were around. Tongue in cheek, we invited Olive and her friend to go sleigh riding with us. I'm sure it was about the wildest sleigh ride that stranger ever had. We took good care of Olive, but how we roughed up that older suitor of hers! We started out smoothly, but we ended by steering the sleigh into a big snowdrift, upsetting it, and pinning the poor fellow in the wagon box we'd fixed up on the sleigh. Ted and I pretended we couldn't lift the box after trying hard, and went for a pole to pry it loose from him. We didn't hurry going after the pole. You can bet your life the older man left for his part of the country the next day, and Ted and I were happy to see him go.

There was always the hardship of not having enough money when it came to courting a girl. Take the basket socials held to raise money for some worthy cause. Each girl packed a basket with tasty items of her own handiwork and the baskets were then auctioned off to the highest bidder who got the privilege of sharing the contents of the basket with the girl. They not only ate together but were paired off for the rest of the evening's festivities. One evening at one of these basket socials I was fit to be tied—I was not expecting any trouble getting my girl's basket, but a rough-looking, rich old bachelor had eyes for my girl and the basket she had so lovingly prepared, and he bid the basket to thirty-five dollars. He got the privilege of eating supper with my girl, and she was obligated to spend the rest of the evening with him, leaving me at loose ends. I learned then that money sure talks. (However, 43 years later I finally did get that girl.)

Girls were scarce in the Old West. As the men moved to the great Western plains, they left the girls where there was more civilization and less danger. I still say the wild open spaces of Montana had advantages, but a man needs the soothing touch of the woman's hand on his tired brow after a rough day on the plains. We recognized that and longed for more of the fair sex out in God's country. If you read the Bible, you know God tells us: "It is not good for man to be alone." Men in old Montana found this very true, and soon there were a few women and girls in the prairie towns.

Men treated the women who ventured into this wilderness with the greatest respect; they practically put the fair sex on a pedestal. Of course the women did not like to be treated like idols. They wanted to be treated like human beings and be allowed to prove they could endure the hardships as well as the men could. The girls I knew soon adapted themselves to the pioneer ways of the Old West. (Olive sure was a wonderful girl!)

SHEEP AND HERDERS

SPRING came, the meadow larks returned, and the grass was just peeping through the land when I went to Stanford on the back of my blaze-faced roan horse. This time I got a job with Bower Brothers on a big sheep ranch on Surprise Creek. I didn't like taking this job because of what my pals from the cow-punching range would think of me—lowering myself to looking after sheep!—but I had to have a job.

I was learning a new business. Bower Brothers had some nice land in the wide valley. There were good buildings on the valley ranch, good camps, and about 40,000 sheep. I liked the men and the boss was all right. Bower Brothers had other ranches too—Home Ranch, Pierce Ranch on Running Wolf Creek, Phillips Ranch, and close to forty camps. I learned about sheep from old sheephands and everything went well.

With the merry month of May came lambing time, when the little new woollies arrive. The grass was quite green then, buttercups blooming along the creeks and the overhanging pussy willows dropping and being replaced by bright green budding leaves.

During lambing time the men were divided into lambing crews and sent out to five different lambing camps. In each camp there was a camp boss, a cook, a lamb-wagon driver, a nightman, a dayman, two bunch herders, a day herder, and good sheds. Montana sheepmen knew they needed this help and equipment; they were the best I ever worked for any place. Each state had its own system of handling sheep, especially at lambing time. I liked the Montana system best, and I have worked in the sheep business in Idaho, California, Washington, and Montana.

Sheep are generally plenty dumb. They'll follow a leader

51

blindly, often to their death. For instance, if one goes over a cutbank or cliff, they'll all follow and pile up, one on top of another. A young ewe will sometimes drop a lamb and not even stop to glance at it. Often the older ewes will act the same way, especially if feed is scarce and they haven't much milk for their babies. This is when a lamber or midwife to sheep has to be a good experienced man.

At lambing time the weather is usually fine; the curlews are coming back and flocks of "honkers" (wild geese) are flying north every day. The drop bands (future mothers) are on the range. The herder takes a band out to graze, and he and a "drop picker" watch carefully; as the lambs are born they're grabbed up with a hook, put into a small pen in the sheep wagon, and then taken quickly to the camp shed and placed in pens just wide enough for mama and her baby or babies to get acquainted.

Don't envy the bunch herder even if he sits a lot, for his hard work comes later. I've seen big men tear their hair, jump up and down, and cuss a lot when it comes time to corral these charges, for as often as not just as he's about to close the gate, one of the sheep will race back to see if she has the right baby. Then the whole crowd will run out after the leader. This means the herder has to do the whole thing over again; so really it's no wonder he loses his temper.

They tell a lot of stories about would-be sheepherders. Here's one tale I like particularly:

"Did you get 'em all in, Gus?"

"Yes sir, you bet I did, but I sure had a tough time on them las' three." The boss then went out to the corral and there in a corner were three of those big Montana jack rabbits. I often wondered if the boss laughed or got angry, for I understand this was a true story.

After a few days with mama, the new lambs are put into the lamb band, which grows larger day by day, and here they stay until they become lamb chops. I don't eat them; prejudiced, I guess.

THE SETTLERS
they came in covered wagons . . .

THE TRAVELERS
they came by stage . . .

THE STORK HOMESTEAD, Montana, 1888
we built a sod house . . .

BOSS OF THE HERDS
the bison is large and quick . . .

SLIM'S GRAVE
he was buried on the lone prairie . . .

STAMPEDE
there was the bawling of cattle, the noise, and the cussing . . .

THE BLANKET STIFF
he was around in 1907 . . .

ONE OF GOD'S CHILDREN
*there were many
deer up there . . .*

THE OLD PROSPECTOR
*and then the storm
whipped up . . .*

BEEF
perhaps they wouldn't be called good beef today . . . .

WHITE-FACED CATTLE
beef clean to the horns . . . .

WARNING NESTORS
the cattlemen did not take kindly to settlers . . .

THE STORYTELLER
his tales enchanted me . . .

SNORT AND BUCK
my horse gave a snort and started to buck . . .

THE SCHOOLMARM'S CABIN
always a popular place . . .

THE OLD SCOUT
tracks spell danger . . .

THE LONE SHEPHERD
the herder takes the band out to graze . . .

THE FIRST FURROW
the sodbuster plowed up the prairie sod . . .

COWBOY REVERIE
he sings to them dogies there under the stars . . .

THE POSSE
*they found the bodies of the Kurts and Briggs
families at Samples Crossing, north of Lewistown . . .*

THE CREEK
it was a beautiful place with a creek close by . . .

JUST A LITTLE STAGE TOWN
Geyser, Montana . . .

THE LONELY LIFE
the sheep were out in the summer camps . . .

TROUBLE
the kind we called a headbuster . . .

OUT WHERE THE WIND
BLOWS FREE
*about the fastest thing
on feet—antelope . . .*

ETERNAL HOPE
Old Tom King and his mule . . .

SOME WOBBLIES
they were around in 1909 . . .

LICE CHIEF
*ohn Sullivan, "a hard man to
eal with," shot by someone . . .*

VIOLENCE EVERY DAY
*Henry Buchel, his jaw
broken in an IWW fray
in Spokane in 1909 . . .*

EVANGELIST
*Sister Bilkiss and her flag,
jailed in* 1909 . . .

WOBBLY QUEEN
*Elizabeth Gurley Flynn
in* 1909 . . .

HOME
it was a neat-looking little house on Howard Street, Spokane . . .

POP'S PRIDE AND JOY
the 1922 Overland . . .

THE FIRST MRS. STORK

I got a nice letter from Ethel Pomeroy . . .

OLLIE SCOTT STORK

Ollie sure was a nice girl . . .

SMELTER SMOKESTACK
there she stood in Great Falls, like a protecting angel, 506 feet high . . .

THE LOST PROSPECTOR
John H. Pomeroy, found in 1944 after 44 years of searching . . .

RAWHIDE SHORTY TODAY

BYRON CLAUDE STORK

A MONTANA BLIZZARD

It was about the twentieth of May, 1903, if my memory serves me right. One night we corralled and all was well. Lonesome Joe, a grizzled old herder, spat on the grass, then looked up at Old Square Butte in the distance, and said, "We's goin' to have snow, Shorty." I still wonder who told him, because it certainly did—and in the merry month of May, the month of spring flowers. The next morning there was about a foot of snow on the ground and it was still coming down with a fierce cold wind right out of the north, a wind that hit and stung the face like a sharp knife.

Things looked pretty serious for all those little woollies out in the open; besides the effect the cold might have on the poor lambs, their mothers wouldn't have fresh grass to eat, and if we fed the mothers dry hay many of them wouldn't have enough milk for their offsprings and would forsake them. The storm also meant the danger of pile-ups, lost sheepherders, bad roads, and other unfortunate things that can happen in a bad storm such as they sometimes have in Montana.

The men were plenty glum as they sat around the big table in the cookhouse eating breakfast that morning. We were all thinking how the sheep could get lost and maybe freeze to death on the great stretches of unfenced prairie and snow-covered trails. Many of the sheep were in summer camps with nothing but a tent and corral near them on the open plains, or at best a hill or water hole.

Mr. Taylor, our camp boss, gave orders and plenty of them. Slim and I had to haul and scatter hay in several different camps, one of the easy jobs. Guess luck was on our side, but

Lord, how fast everybody worked! The "drop bands" had to be held in the shed and all work connected with it done there. No midwife ever worked as hard as those sheephands did all through the storm. It went on snowing harder and harder all that day. The temperature continued to drop and that cold biting wind got worse every hour.

We didn't get to bed until very late that night and we were all hoping things would be better in the morning. Vain hope! It was far worse in the morning, with great drifts around the sheds and corrals. Red Nelson, the bunch herder, came in with frozen toes, and I got a frost blister on my nose. It looked like a big wart, and the men told me not to break it, but I was getting cross-eyed looking at it, so I dabbed it with alcohol, stuck a needle into it, and it went down fast.

Calvin Bower, one of the ranch owners, arrived on an inspection trip. He came over to me and asked, "You know the trail to Arrow Creek, don't you? How'd you like to go out there with me?"

"Yes, I know the trail," I replied. "I don't think the ride will be any vacation, but I'll go."

We started out on the trail after I finished the chores the boss had assigned to me. We rode down Surprise Creek and across the benchlands and coulees in a buckboard. Mr. Bower had a team of young black geldings I sure wished I could have on my Tiger Butte homestead.

Mr. Bower began bragging about the fine loyal bunch of men he had working for him. He said a bad storm like this one sure tested us all. But soon we had other things to talk about. We got into a big drift when we ran off the trail and nearly upset, and to make matters worse one of the horses got the line under his tail and clamped down hard. I leaped out of the buckboard and got the line free as the horses plowed and dragged the sharply tipped rig. Mr. Bower's coat caught just as he left the buckboard and he was dragged a few feet through the deep snow. I finally succeeded in getting hold of the other line and stopped the team.

We were covered with snow, we even had it inside our clothes; but I was used to snow and didn't mind it too much. I just shook it out of my bear skin overcoat and then quickly buttoned the coat up to my neck again to shut out as much of the cold wind as possible. Mr. Bower went through the same procedure with his fine buffalo skin coat, but he'd had a bit of hard luck. He'd lost one of his mittens in the drift and we couldn't find it, so we had to make a sort of mitten out of an old rag we found in the buckboard. Now it was up to me to do the driving.

Mr. Bower soon began to complain about the cold. "Shorty, you can sure take it, I'm about frozen." He was stamping his feet on the floor of the buckboard and clapping his hands together to keep the circulation going.

I answered him, "We're near the Jack Scott camp. There's wood there. We'd better try an' find the cabin an' warm up before we go on any further. We won't find any grub, though, for it's a summer camp."

We reached the cabin in a short time, and built ourselves a brisk fire in the old wood stove, but when we came out of the cabin, the trail was completely covered and the wind was howling as if to say, "Go home, you damn fools, or I'll get you yet!"

I knew the hills in this country and usually couldn't get lost, but this time we did get lost, and after wandering around in the snow for several hours, we found we had backtracked. We came upon our own wagon tracks. The situation was pretty serious; it was growing dark and we should have reached Arrow Creek long before this.

We decided to try something different. I began walking ahead of the team until I was nearly out of sight of it, then Mr. Bower drove up to me and I walked on again. We did this for quite a while, and just before dark I saw a point of rock I recognized. Then the storm whipped up again and I lost the rock.

Mr. Bower yelled to me, "Shorty, I heard a sheep bleat. Go to the right!"

"Yes, I hear it, but I'm sure it's way over to the left an' in front of us."

"You're wrong!" he insisted, so there we were. He was boss and what he said was always right. I wondered what to do.

Then we heard a faint sound distinctly from the left and the boss said to go that way. We were both discouraged, hungry, and chilled clean through. It seemed to me Mr. Bower was getting a little woozy; or maybe it was me, I thought. I was more than a little frightened as the snow curled up all around us. It seemed we might both freeze stiff out here in the wilds.

I slapped the lines over the horses' rumps and it wasn't long before something loomed ahead. It was the prettiest sight I'd ever seen: a lone lighted lantern hanging by a sheep corral! The light shone dimly through the blizzard, but it meant we were safe.

The herder at the corral was sure glad to see us. If any man needed help he did. He told us all the trouble he had been having and said, "I was afraid to go to bed, 'cause some of those woolies will pile up an' how if they ain't stirred 'round once in a while; they always does in th' snow, yuh know." We both gave him credit for sticking by his job so well.

The herder fixed us hot coffee and some chuck, and we began to feel right human again. In fact, I started feeling pretty drowsy, but I fought it off, knowing there'd be no sleep for me that night. Mr. Bower, the herder, and I took turns keeping the sheep from piling up; we all worked hard at the job until daybreak.

By morning the storm had eased somewhat but it was still awfully cold. I was sure lucky I could stay in the warm cabin, but Mr. Bower declared he couldn't waste any more time, so he started out in the cold through the deep snowdrifts. He had a tough time getting through the drifts that day, and just barely made it.

The blizzard acted as if it had only stopped long enough to get strength to howl again, for soon the snow began coming down in a howling wind. The storm went on. It continued without letup for five days and five nights. We had no thermometer at the corral, but I learned later that we'd lived through some real bitter cold—it had been forty degrees below zero!

The sun came out after the fifth day and shone brightly, as if to mend all the damage the storm had caused, and let me tell you there was plenty of damage! There had been a great loss of all kinds of stock, but it was the sheep that were hardest hit. Six herders froze to death in Cascade County. Flying creatures couldn't take it either, for when the snow melted clusters of small birds were found in the brush—all of them dead. Yes, weather can be tough in Montana.

This was only one of the many blizzards I lived through in Montana. I remember the hard winter in 1890 when a number of sheepherders froze to death, and the terrible winter of 1886 finished off nearly all the great tough kings of the prairie—the bison or buffalo.

Bower Brothers made me foreman and put me on the Pierce Ranch south of Stanford. My job was to irrigate, tend camp for one sheep band, handle haying crews, etc. My three-room cabin was on a beautiful site with a creek on two sides of it, and Dry Wolf Creek near the mountains was close by. I had two saddle horses, a team, wagon, buckboard, and the usual camp equipment.

Plenty of fish could be had any time I wanted to go fishing, and I could go to town any time I wanted to, which was generally in the evenings when there was always a big poker game going on. I played occasionally (I hadn't learned my lesson yet, that is, a winner eventually loses). I've seen many a sheepherder and cowhand start for Great Falls with a year's wages or more, stop in Stanford, and lose every cent there in the poker games. The games were plenty exciting because the stakes were high, but I learned my lesson early, and am glad I don't have to go through that experience again.

Up in the hills there was quite a lively rattlesnake population. I skinned a few—killed 'em first, I can tell you! Skins made nifty hatbands, and some of the boys liked the rattlers' skins made into fancy belts. The rattlers killed a lot of stock. In the Great Falls locale some people were bitten, but few fatally. Once I got a real scare. I was walking along barefooted when I stepped on something soft. I didn't stop to examine what it was but just jumped fast. Then I looked back to see the biggest rattler I have ever seen. I sure was lucky it wasn't coiled at the time.

Haying time on the Pierce Ranch ended, and, according to the law, I had to go back to my homestead for six months. I returned to my place and batched it there for the time required, doing a few odd jobs around my ranch and getting a few paying jobs too. For entertainment I went to the dances in town once in a while.

The most popular girls with the cowboys and ranchers were the schoolmarms, and I liked them too. Trouble was, there weren't enough schoolmarms to go around. The schoolmarm's cabin was a pretty popular place on Saturdays, and every evening a half dozen horses could be seen chomping at the bit out by her hitching post.

In the late eighties and early nineties there were no school teachers out in the wilds; therefore my education was sorely neglected for quite some time. Later, however, when the country began to fill up, I did go to school. But I got nothing beyond fourth-grade learning and that when it was too late to give me much more than a smattering of the three R's.

But everybody gets a heap of learning just by living their lives. My life has been a long one, so I feel I've got a lot of learning in my head that real experience has taught me. I know plenty about many things a man could never find in textbooks, good things I can tell about and pass on to others by putting paint on a canvas.

I spent the required six months on my homestead, and then for a time worked for a small cattle outfit south of Stockett. They were building up a herd by buying orphan calves. One day the boss took me into Stockett to get two calves he'd heard were for sale. We made the trip by buckboard on a cold winter day and when we arrived at the cabin where we were to find the calves, I was chilled to the bone.

But the worst was yet to come! We went into the cabin and talked the purchase over with the owner, and he said, "Sure, you can have the calves at five dollars apiece. They're out in the woodshed." The boss sent me out to the shed to get the calves. I found two fine husky fellows tied to a post by a tub of water. I stooped over and grabbed one in my arms. This calf sure took the cake as far as the kicking went; he put up a big kick for his freedom. I hung onto him but took a step back to balance myself—and went *kerflop* into that tub of icy water with the squirming, kicking calf right in my lap. The water soaked into my shoes and my pants were mighty uncomfortable. A cat peacefully drinking milk out of a saucer nearby got scared and leaped on the back of the other calf. The calf broke the rope holding it and leaped out an open window. During all this, I was making frantic efforts to get the first calf off my lap, but it stuck like glue in spite of its twisting and plunging, soaking me from top to bottom.

I was just congratulating myself that nobody was seeing my miserable predicament when the shed door was opened and there stood the new schoolmarm, the last person I wanted to see! She gave me a strange look and said primly, "Such a peculiar place to bathe!" She tried to disappear as quickly as she had come, but the calf in my lap had other ideas. It leaped up and made for the door. Now calf and schoolmarm attempted to be first through the open door, but it wasn't wide enough, and the calf made it first. I attempted to blabber an apology, but with my shoes squishing and water pouring out of my pants, I was such a comical-looking character that the pretty girl laughed and laughed. From this time on I was the butt of many pointed remarks about my ability to handle calves and the odd places in which I chose to take a bath.

Weekends usually found me down on the Scott place in the Red Butte district. A good time was had by all at the Scott Ranch, but heck, I could never see Ollie (Olive) Scott alone. There was always a bunch of saddle horses tied to the Scott fence, which meant there was a bunch of cowboys and ranchers inside the house.

Ollie could sure play the organ that stood in the parlor, and she would sing in the sweetest voice to her own playing. Her singing was easily worth the long trip we boys made to visit her. We generally ended up playing some silly card game and it was quite a trick to get one of those Scott girls for a partner, but someone had to win out and sometimes I did. I always thought Ollie gave me an edge—but I wasn't sure. I had great plans for her and me and hoped, like the old song said, that "We'd Never Change Partners Again."

I was always pretty conscientious about my work, but sometimes I guess I was too independent. One time I was working for a well-to-do rancher. I liked the job and the pay, but one day when we were fencing and I was tamping the posts, I caught the boss trying to shake the posts and I got a little cocky. I snapped, "Mister, don't you think you can trust me to do a good job?"

"Well, after all, I'm paying for the job," he snapped back. "Guess I can try these posts to see if they'll stand."

"You sure can!" I flung back at him. "Here are the tools! You can set all these damn posts yourself! I'll be back tomorrow for the pay you owe me." I slammed the tools on the ground and walked off the place. My silly independence cost me a job, and I had to start looking for another one.

THIS AND THAT

OLD TIGER BUTTE was losing its snowcap. Once again it was spring and time for me to leave my homestead and all the fun and work of batching there. I was young and confident and it was with high hopes that I saddled old Pat, my blaze-faced sorrel, and hit for Utica in Fergus County.

When I reached town and went into the Morris and Waite Saloon to get warm, the first person I saw was grizzled old Tom King, a gold prospector. He was all aglow with eagerness to hit the trail to his diggings high up on Baldy Mountain, and just had to have somebody to talk to. We were standing by the pot-bellied stove where I was warming my hands when I heard a familiar voice, "Why Shorty! Hello! How are you?"

I looked around and there stood Sandy McGregor, blacksmith from the Bower Ranch. We were glad to see each other again and after a couple of drinks at the bar, Sandy learned I was looking for a job. He told me Walter Waite, co-partner of the saloon, needed an extra man on his ranch.

Sandy took me out to the Waite Ranch and introduced me to Walter, telling him, "I know Shorty. He's okay, just the man you're lookin' for."

Walter asked me a few questions, then he tossed one that kind of stopped me: "Can you break a team of mules?" I hesitated for a moment; I wanted that job, still I wanted to be honest too. "I'd sure like to try," I evaded carefully. So I learned about mules!

Walter showed me the mules, two wild-eyed, lively, long-eared gentlemen, dangerous at both ends when they wanted to be. I was then taken to see the cattle and about 125 head of horses, ten brood mares, and hundreds of chickens. Walter owned eight hundred acres on Sage Creek and lots of open range near the mountains. He also owned a sheep camp. His cook was quite a character, but nice enough when sober, which wasn't often.

Walter sent men out here to work when they couldn't pay their whisky bills in his saloon. I told Walter this was bad management. He grinned and asked, "Don't you drink, kid?"

"Oh, maybe one or two now and then. I know when to quit —I think whisky makes fools of men."

He looked surprised and said, "Maybe so—maybe so, kid."

I could see he had something special on his mind, and finally it came out. "Think you could run this place, Shorty? There's seventy-five dollars a month in it."

"Seems to me you'd better keep your present man," I said, for I didn't want to see anybody lose their job because of me. But I went on and said, "I think I could improve on some things around here."

Walter looked at me and said, "The job's yours, Shorty."

Here I was with a new job, but there was that team of unbroken mules to reckon with. I knew general ranch experience would help some. Walter had a nice layout here: good sheds, fine water, and plenty of grass. This was really a beautiful part of the country. Everywhere the eyes strayed beauty could be seen.

The mules and I gradually got acquainted, and it wasn't long before I had them halter-broke and could lead them to water. I led them snubbed to a horse until they were halter-broke, then I finally hitched one at a time to a wagon and tied over to a big old mare that was able to hold them down. I tied the whole outfit to a snubbing post, and when in the wagon by myself, I yanked on the rope and it came loose. I said, "Get up!" and those mules sure did get up and take off the first few times, but I expected a fast ride and was prepared.

I soon had the mules tame enough so I could put them together on the wagon without the old mare, and then I had a dandy team. I named them Jack and Jim, and they sure were a couple of black beauties. In no time at all they became my pets. I knew then the old-timer was right when he said, "Mules has got sense."

Everything went pretty smoothly on the Waite Ranch, but when fall came, I got another hand to take my place until spring. I had to get back to my homestead to comply with the law.

At the homestead I found an interesting letter. I was offered a chance to go on a cattle drive to Billings, then by train to Chicago, and back to Montana. I didn't want to miss that, so I hurried off to Utica and joined the outfit. Slim McCarthy was along too, and it seemed like old times being with friends, cattle, and a chuck wagon.

Our outfit proved to be the tail-end of several herds, all beef, mostly steers. We left from a little north of Utica, where they'd been bedded down the night before. The boys had good horses, and I had one for my own use. It was a great morning when we started out with the sun popping up in the east and the sky clear and blue all around and the air with that wonderful early morning mountain freshness.

We had a time trying to hold the cattle back so they wouldn't run all the meat off their bones before we could deliver them. There was one old bobtailed cow that caused us plenty of trouble. She was what the cowpokes call a headbuster, a bobtailed critter. Her tail had been either frozen off or partly chewed off by coyotes. It was dangerous to get near such animals. When a man got hit on the head by a bobtail, he felt like a sandbag had banged him, and he was sometimes out cold for a few minutes.

Cattle, like people, have different personalities, and troublesome characters crop up pretty often on long drives. But on this drive all seemed to be going well until the cattle began crowding together as if danger threatened. The next thing we knew, we saw a wolf run out of a clump of brush, but luckily one of our men was quick on the trigger, and when the wolf lay dead on the ground the cattle cooled down and on we went on our drive.

Slim's main topic of conversation while we were riding along was how much fun we'd have in Chicago, where poker stakes were high and the girls had more class than those in Montana.

"Then they must be pretty classy," I remarked.

"Yep, they sure is."

We made a dry camp early the first night because we didn't want to crowd the cattle and we had a long drive yet to Billings where we were to load. It was a quiet night and all went well. After supper we sat around the campfire and swapped yarns. Somehow the subject turned to religion, which was an unusual one for a cow camp. Some of the boys had heard and liked the singing and preaching of Brother Van (W.W. Van Orsdale). He would preach anywhere, any time, and he said he loved everybody, but that didn't stop him from telling people about the evil in their ways. Slim said, "Brother Van's no sissy either; he can fight when it's necessary."

"I know," I put in. "He's fought with the Indians, I hear, an' they approve of him—which is odd."

Yes, Brother Van had sung his way up the Missouri River to Fort Benton in 1872. He was just a kid preacher then; he always got around on horseback, by buckboard, or stage. He didn't care how he traveled and he traveled hundreds of miles to carry the Lord's message. He became the "range boss"— presiding elder of Central Montana's Methodist Church. Maybe we cowpunchers liked preachers because we needed them so bad.

Utica had another preacher everybody liked. This Rev. John Rogers got kicked by a horse and the injury was fatal, an odd way for a preacher to die, I grant you. The whole town closed up business the day of the burial, and everybody attended the funeral. That was Montana for you in the old days.

We were all up early next morning and, as usual, Old Headbuster was bent on showing us where to go, but we showed her different. However, a hotbox on our chuckwagon slowed us down. I guess sand got in the wheels; anyway we had to stop and jack up the wagon and pour water on the hubs of the wheels, then wait for them to cool, grease them plenty, and hope they'd stay fixed till we got to our destination.

The cook stood around looking worried when the wagon tipped. He said, "Boys, if you want any more bread, don't spill that sourdough." You can bet your life we were careful with that sourdough, for we all liked that cook's bread.

We drove until dusk, then we made another dry camp and let the dogies fill up on grass again. We had our chuck and we had our usual session around the campfire. It's grand to sit around a campfire and talk, with all the punchers full of bragging and high ideas. Sitting around the fire at night does something great to a man—yes, except when it rains.

STAMPEDE

I WAS LOOKING at the fancy pictures the campfire was making and listening to the talk, now and then taking part in the conversation, when the boss came up and said, "Sorry to disturb you, Shorty, but it's your turn to watch them dogies till it's twelve midnight by the stars. Then Slim can take over. Let's all roll in, fellers; we've got a long, hot, dusty way to go tomorrow."

I went out under the stars and began singing to the dogies, but they didn't seem to appreciate my good voice. They were acting restless, especially Old Bobtail Headbuster. She was about every place at once and as nervous as any cow I'd ever seen. I thought to myself, maybe she didn't like so much male company.

I heard a coyote howl in the distance and I thought maybe Old Headbuster would run like a coyote if she got the chance, but she just went on looking and acting a little too wild, but not really doing anything bad.

Sounds are magic in the night; even the breeze sighs as it comes down the coulee, sounding like some strange monster held in a cage. A lonely hoot owl put in his nickel's worth, and it combined with my singing like a band I once heard in Great Falls. I looked up at the stars and watched the Big Dipper circle the North Star, and I knew it was about time for Slim to get out here.

Soon he came up, singing softly so he wouldn't scare the dogies and make them take off in a mad rush.

He said, "Mornin', Shorty! How goes it?"

I answered him very softly, "So far okey, though you'd

better keep an eye on Old Headbuster; she's been acting kinda wild."

Slim's laugh was careless. "Don't you worry none. I know how to get on with them old ladies. You better go an' git yourself some sleep."

I needed no second invitation, for I was very tired. When I reached camp it was dark and quiet. I just grabbed myself a cup of java off the cold camp stove, drank it fast, and then rolled up in my blanket, and boy, did it feel nice and cozy.

I thought I must be dreaming when somebody tore off my blanket and began giving orders. "Shorty! Wake up! Get on your horse quick—go out to the herd an' help turn 'em! It's a stampede!"

I managed to get to my feet. I heard a great rumbling noise and felt the ground shake. I didn't wait to pull on socks, just yanked on my boots, ran for Old Pat and flung myself on his back, and we hit it for the east side of the roaring, running bunch of cattle. It was still dark and I couldn't see much but shadows and sparks of fire made by clashing horns. I could hear their horns clicking and rattling as they ran into each other. Up ahead some of the boys were yelling and I tried to get their direction from the sounds. I wanted to join them, but I got hemmed in by stampeding animals, and all I could do was keep the stragglers in line.

Old Pat stepped into a badger hole and fell, but luckily I didn't get ditched. When we ran through a thorn bush I got my big toe pinned to my boot, but I didn't stop and tend to it then for things were really moving fast.

The cattle finally began slowing down and I saw a streak of light in the far east of the Snowy Mountains. I came to the conclusion the boys had succeeded in turning back the cattle, but I still could hear them cursing and swearing. I raced ahead and found them—that is, all except Slim.

The boss greeted me, "Glad you're all right, Shorty. Wonder where Slim is." Nobody seemed to know. We still had work to do so we couldn't take time to go back over the trail and look for him right then. We worked for quite a while getting the cattle all bunched together. Then the discussion got back to Slim. The boss said, "Come on, Shorty an' Pinkie—let's go back an' see if we can find Slim." There was a sort of fear in his voice, the same kind I was feeling.

The three of us began riding back across the now quiet prairie. Suddenly Pinkie pointed a shaking finger and said, "What's that over there by that badger hole?" All three of us knew what it was before we got any closer. I started saying a little prayer, thinking at the same time maybe I was asking God to do the impossible. Well, there he was, poor Slim with his neck busted. We had to shoot his horse with the broken legs, and I saw the boss close his eyes when he pulled the trigger.

The boss wouldn't believe Slim was dead. He said to me, "Take my horse, Shorty, an' ride fast to Lewistown. Bring the doctor back here, get Dr. Hedges!" I did just that, but it did no good. The doctor gave one look at poor Slim and said, "He's done." The boys in our outfit chipped in and paid the doctor. This was the least we could do for our old buddy.

We took Slim's body back to the burying place on the lone prairie by the stage road. The boss read the Lord's Prayer and we all stood by and cried. We would miss Slim, a right good friend; he was a square-shooter with everyone. (Later on this burying place on the river side of the road east of Philbrook became the Philbrook Cemetery.)

On the way back to where we had left the cattle, I got to thinking about how Slim loved a joke, not so much the kind played on him, but the ones he played on the other fellow. For instance, the time in Stanford when he played a joke on Dirty Jim, a sheepherder. We worked on him until we got him dead drunk. Then when he passed out, we shaved off his five years' growth of beard. Dirty Jim finally regained his senses, and he did rave when he discovered his beard was gone. Slim and I stood around pretending to feel sorry for him, and I guess we looked so damn innocent poor Dirty Jim never did suspect Slim and I were the ones he ought to hate.

Another time Slim and I tucked Limburger cheese inside the hatband of Dusty, one of the riders in our outfit. The smell nearly drove Dusty nuts. He finally got rid of the cheese, but even washing his hat in the creek didn't make it smell sweeter, so in desperation he rode into town and bought himself a new Stetson. Dusty wasn't too mad over this little joke, or at least he didn't show any anger, but he was the silent type and didn't show his feelings much.

We rode slowly back to the camp and the cattle. Now we had to wait and let the cattle regain the pounds they'd lost on their wild rampage. We traveled slowly. The weather was fine and we lived well on our slow journey. We got an antelope near the crossing on Swimming Woman Creek. Our cook was exceptional, a pretty good man with a gun, and we had prairie chicken feeds very often on the trip.

For several days after the stampede we were a solemn-faced bunch of fellows, but time has a way of easing things, although I thought of Slim often, of his hearty laugh and his sense of humor.

Finally we reached Billings, loaded, and went by train to Chicago, where the lights were bright and the ladies fair. But I decided I preferred God's open country lighted by the stars, moon, and sun overhead, and I longed to get back to Montana where the girls ride and rope with the best of them.

When I got back to my homestead, I was too happy to mind the mice and pack rats that had taken over. I pitched in and, really working, soon had things righted again, and went back to my old way of living on the homestead. I hunted jack rabbits and prairie chickens and spent some time visiting around the neighborhood. I also went to a few dances.

This part of the country around Logging Creek was pretty rough. I heard about a man who cut himself badly with his axe while getting timber for the mines at Neihart. Since it was impossible for his partner to carry him into own, he left him bundled up and rode off to fetch the doctor. But by the time the partner and the doctor returned, they came upon a horrible sight. The injured man was dead; wolves had gnawed him to the bone.

We usually got our supplies in Great Falls, forty miles away, and on my way to Great Falls I had to wait over in Stockett for the train. During this wait, I went down to the "bad lands," the district where the drinks were. I just wanted to pass a few hours while waiting for the train, and I did just that, in addition to wasting some of my hard-earned money.

I didn't drink, but I got into a little poker game. One man won consistently until he had thirty-five dollars of my money. Thank goodness I had to quit then, as my train was due any minute. But before I got out of town I had a few minutes to talk with the man who had won my money.

I asked him, "Partner, what's your line of business?"

After looking me over very thoroughly, he answered, "Who, me? I'm a sheepherder."

I gave him a knowing wink. "Yes, and what else?" I wanted to let him know I was on to him.

Gambling sharks were going it strong even in those days. Barnum used to say, "A sucker is born every minute." This surely is true so far as gambling is concerned.

ETERNAL HOPE

HERE IS a picture of my old prospector friend, Tom King of Utica, Montana. Like most prospectors, he was honest, self-reliant, and always hopeful. "Eternal hope," I called it. While I was foreman on Walter Waite's mixed cattle and sheep ranch up in the hills in the Little Belt Mountains southwest of Utica in about 1903, I came to know Tom well.

It was spring again and the pussy willows were beginning to come out. The woods were all atwitter with bird songs, and the remnants of winter's snowdrifts were lying here and there in shady places under the trees. Tom, happy as a lark, was off for the hills for the twentieth time. His shaggy gray locks hung down almost to his shoulders and curled up neatly at the back of his head, just like a drake's tail. His countenance was all aglow with hope, and good nature beamed from his bright blue eyes. He wore a big high hat that looked somewhat the worse for wear. His wrinkled old neck, like old buckskin leather slightly tinted, was somewhat bent, as if to brace against the wind, the wind he had faced for many years when spring came and the grass started turning green and the meadow larks began to sing.

"Yes sir, boys, we got her in the bag for sure this time," he soliloquized, tightening the cinch on his pack mule and snubbing the halter rope to his saddle mule's tail. How he did love his mules! They were at once his faithful servants and loyal friends. After getting into the saddle, he waved goodbye to the bystanders. They waved back, calling out, "So long, Tom, be seeing you in the fall. Bring us some of those yellow boys," meaning nuggets, of course.

71

So around the bend they trotted, frying pans and tools beating a merry tune as they fared forth on the trail leading up into the heights of the Little Belt Mountains in Central Montana, where each year Tom was sure he would find the source of coarse gold and "nuggets like pigeon eggs." Up the trail he went, over the hills and through the forest, past the old hunter's cabin by the spring, where he exchanged greetings with him, the last white man he would see for a considerable time. That didn't bother Tom any, for as he always said, "Mules is good company. They talks to them as will understand 'em."

When he got around the bend his work started. There across the trail was a big tree that had fallen during the winter. Talking to the mules, he said, "Boys, the work starts here for me; you lucky fellows can eat while I work." He unstrapped his crosscut saw and looked up and saw something waddle out of a clump of brush and bear grass into a cluster of aspens. He said, "Well, there goes ol' Porky an' he sure looks fat." Porky was a porcupine, and experienced mountain men do not molest them.

He worked hard and removed the tree, and then resumed his long, tiresome journey. The trail led up, always upward, upward through mossy rock outcroppings that nature had painted with many colors. The sun got higher, and it was quite warm when they came to a spring gurgling out of the rocks by the yellow pine. The water crossed the trail and it was here they camped for dinner. Tom visited with the mules. "Yes sir, javy 'n bacon, 'n don't you go lookin' fer bars an' sech." Mules and bears are not on speaking terms. While the mules grazed peacefully, Tom took a pail to get water from the spring. Suddenly a flock of blue grouse rose with a noise that startled him slightly, and flew away with that zigzag motion for which they are noted, through the trees and over a rise in the hills.

Dinner over, Tom and his mules went up the trail, over the hills and around bends, each of which offered a new panorama, for there was always life of some kind. The antelope scurried around the hill and swiftly disappeared in the distance as they went to lower country.

Tom stopped and looked at the hitches on the pack mule he called Ol' Lightnin'. The mule was a veteran of many pack trains and was fully trail-wise. As they were about to start again, Ol' Lightnin' gave a short snort, and Pete, the saddle mule, raised his head suddenly and looked up the trail. Tom spoke to the mules, "What you fellers lookin' fer anyway? Well, I'll be durned, you's right, those bars is out early. Thar they go." A black mother bear and two yearlings crossed the trail and went leisurely down the hill. The mules still looked after them but slowly quieted down. Around another bend they went and abruptly there, shining and shimmering in the distance, was Old Baldy. Tom pointed to the mountain. "That'll be home fer us this summer. Thar's good grass thar an' meat, an' thar's gold thar too, sez I."

It was getting dusk now, and as they came around a big rock that had a tree growing out of its side, Tom saw an ideal camping spot. Some trees had fallen and made a natural corral, and there was water cascading down into the valley from a spring. "Wal, fellers, here we camps fer the night an' you can fill your bellies on thet thar grass an' be happy." He stripped the pack and saddle and turned the mules out to roll in the grass, which they immediately did, shaking themselves with gusto before they started to feed. Tom put the hobbles on Ol' Lightnin' and went about making an open camp.

"Sure is sumpin' soothin' an' happy about the smell of bacon an' hot java out here in the hills, I sez." Supper over, Tom built a little fire and sat there talking to himself and philosophizing. "God sure made things big 'n good like all those stars up thar. Wonder what makes 'em stick to their places. Such lots of them too." The mules heaved sighs of contentment and Ol' Lightnin' lay down to rest. Tom took his blankets and a tarpaulin and made a bed by a big tamarack log that lay close to the trail. Then he bedded down and watched the stars blink till he passed into dreamland where the gold was always in the pan and meat on the table.

Golden dawn was just streaking the east when Tom was awakened by a flock of quail filing slowly over the log by his head. "Looks like they's goin' ter breakfus' an' I is too," Tom said, as he put the blankets over the log to let the sun thaw the light frost that had fallen on them during the night. Just then three big blacktail deer came dashing out of the trees and down the trail. Tom mused, "Cougar maybe; them cats is no good, I sez." He looked after the fleeing deer and continued, "Them deer is sure scared as all get-out."

Breakfast over, Tom took a couple of pieces of salt out to the mules, talked to each of them, and got some water. "Mules and men have got ter drink, don't they, boys? I mean water, of of course." Then they headed up the trail as the sun painted peak after peak a golden yellow and the long purple shadows on the crags and peaks slowly disappeared. Now they were among trees and flowers and ferns, then past colored rocks where the mica gleamed in the sun like gold and spring after spring came trickling down from the hills as the snow slowly melted in the golden sun.

Noon came, and camp time. Tom patted the sweating mules and removed their loads. "We got ter take it easy 'cause we want ter get thar with meat on these bones so's to locate that lode in the hill. An' we're just the fellers that can do it, eh boys?" Tom got dinner after shooting a grouse, and the mules fed on the tall lush grass until they had their fill. Then Tom said, "We just got ter hit the trail agin so's ter get thar before dark." He tightened the cinch and adjusted the load for the last long upward lap of their journey to Old Baldy Mountain gleaming and shimmering above. The mountain looked like burnished silver.

The afternoon sun made the trail hot and dusty, and Tom had to clear away a windfall every little while or cut a sapling that crowded the trail, so the packs could get by. Once they had to disturb a rotting log and a cloud of insects arose. "Yellow jackets," said Tom, "Let's hurry, fer these boys shore have hot feet, an' that's fer sure."

The sun was getting lower and the shadows of the stunted and twisted trees were lengthened as they approached timber line. A flock of fool hens went strutting by, but Tom had no time to pot one, for it would soon be dark. A woodpecker stopped beating his tattoo on a tree by the trail; he screeched and flew away. A hoot owl in the distance was hooting his call of the wild. Tom and his mules passed through a copse of small pines, and there before them loomed a cabin by a spring that came tumbling over the gravel and boulders. The first stars of evening were just peeping through as they arrived.

The little dirt-roofed cabin looked about as it had when Tom and the mules had departed the previous fall, except that the door was partly open.

Tom unsaddled and unpacked, turning the mules out to roll. "Yep, they rolled three times, in Missouri. A mule is worth one hundred dollars if he rolls three times." The mules were happy. This was home to them, and after shaking vigorously, they went to grazing.

"You boys is lucky, yer supper's ready, but I got to cook mine yet. Better see what home looks like inside; pack rats, I bet a million," he said, as he pulled the door the rest of the way open. Being a man of experience, he gingerly stepped back a distance. Old lady skunk walked out slowly and with dignity, followed by two baby skunks, and they passed out of sight by the spring. Tom waited quietly in the shadows until they passed, saying to himself, "All who knows them kitties real well respects them, I sez; I does, anyway."

He went inside the cabin very cautiously, sniffing the air; it was musty and humid and smelled of rats. "I guess we won't disturb them pack rats tonight. Lucky for me that mama skunk didn't get excited and spill inside the cabin. Yep, I get supper an' sleep outside ternight; but outside the smell that cabin is sure homelike an' peaceful. I got ter get diggin' early 'cause the season is short up here."

Tom sat by the fire after supper and dreamed of gold and all it could get for him: "We sure got her in the bag this time. Those colors mean sumpin' an' it's gold. Yes sir, an' that rock was gettin' softer. That last shot last fall showed signs. Yes sir, we'll git her uncovered soon!" Finally he rolled into his blankets. The last sound he heard was a mourning dove in the distance sighing, "Ooooo! Ooooo! He, ho, ho!"

With the coming of morning, Tom bagged himself a deer, ate his breakfast, did a little house cleaning, and went to work in his prospect hole. First there was a cave-in to clear away. This took two days. Then it was drill and shoot, inspect and shoot again, and so all summer long—but to no avail, only a few streaks of red in the rock. All he got were "signs" and more "signs."

Late in the season he went out to the mules and held a conference. "Guess we better go down an' pan the creek where we's sure ter get sumpin', 'cause men and mules have got ter eat; ain't thet so fellers?" The mules were in agreement, so Tom panned the creek for weeks. Finally, the weather drove them back to Utica for the winter, just as it had done for twenty years. "But boys, we sure got her in the bag nex' 'year! That last shot uncovered signs and those colors mean sumpin' for sure. Too bad winter comes so early up thar. We'll play solitary fer a few months till the spring sun shines on Old Baldy again. We got 'er in the bag fer sure next summer!"

IT WAS A TIGHT GAME

IN THE OLD WEST people were quite democratic and learned how to cooperate in their problems. One could hardly tell who was boss around most of the ranches and cattle outfits till the boss had occasion to give orders, and then we usually took notice and quickly too, for most of the bosses knew men and cattle, the range and brands well. The boss usually ate with his men in the same cookhouse or chuck wagon, and one thing is sure—we didn't laugh at the boss' jokes as they do now. Bosses of that period just had to be good or else.

I am reminded of the time I worked for Otto Schott at his ranch south of Stockett. One day the president of the Great Falls National Bank (they called it Ford's Bank then) came out to Otto's cabin home for dinner, a bachelor dinner, they called it. That man sure cut loose with jokes and loose talk. One thing he said sticks in my mind; it was: "Well, Otto, I see you don't use finger bowls out here or talk to your plate."

I said, "No, maybe not, but we do talk to the dog and when the dog isn't around we talk to ourselves."

The president thoroughly enjoyed himself and the freedom we had around there without all the niceties and folderol he was accustomed to in the society he moved in in the city. Otto was a bachelor and he had a nice place with about one hundred head of fine beef cattle that winter.

It was cold and there was a lot of snow. I was the hired hand and it was my job to drive the cattle about one and a half miles to water daily, cut the ice, and hold the cattle there until all of them had gotten their drink of water—and, believe me, it was a tough job, because they always took their time, or at least it seemed so to me when that cold wind blew out of the

77

north and it was forty degrees below zero. The wind would nip your nose, yours ears, your cheeks, but it was important that beef cattle got plenty of water.

One day Otto said, "I'll tell you what, Shorty—I'll play you a game of pitch today an' every day to see which of us takes the cattle to the water hole while this cold weather lasts. The loser'll do the driving." Of course this was okay with me as it really was my job.

Those games of pitch sure had something in them. We played almost as if our lives depended on those games. I learned Otto's little tricks and it wasn't long before he had to put on his big bearskin coat, button it to his chin, get those old mitts out, and head that bunch of cattle to the water hole while I, the hired hand, stayed by the nice warm stove and had chuck ready when Otto returned. The pitch game was always nip and tuck, and on the whole about even. Otto was a good boss and a fine manager, and he made money.

PIONEER CHRISTMASES

CHRISTMAS and other holidays were sometimes difficult to celebrate out in the wide open spaces. We all tried to make a celebration, though.

I remember one winter I was working for a cattle outfit that was just starting out. We were forty miles from town. It started to snow heavily and got crusted and cold as all heck. The boss had gone to Great Falls for some grub and he had been gone for several days. Christmas Eve came and I had only my dog for company. At least that was all the company I had inside, but there were plenty of visitors outside that mountain cabin if tracks told anything.

On Christmas Eve I sat there and sang carols to the dog. He was the most appreciative audience I ever had. It was definitely what most people would call a lonely Christmas, but I kept busy with my drawing, and the time passed pleasantly.

The boss didn't get back until spring, and we got to be on very short rations, I can tell you—sourdough flapjacks, except when I got a grouse or pheasant.

There's another interesting Christmas my wife speaks of often. She and her family came from Canada to Fort Benton in 1887 in search of land and a new home. They headed out that long, lonely road to Stanford, which was then a little stage town sixty-two miles from Great Falls.

The party consisted of Mr. and Mrs. Scott; Lillie, age six; Olive, five; Dave, nine; and the baby George, just three. Like most people of those times, they didn't expect the life they were heading into to be easy, and it wasn't. They stopped for a short time with Mr. Scott's brother Jack at Surprise Creek, west of Stanford.

79

Jack had some sheep and was already established in a small way. He had the usual range troubles of the day. One day Bob Scot came to the cabin and, in a matter-of-fact way, put his hand inside his shirt and withdrew it. It was covered with blood. Mrs. Scott wanted to know how he got hurt. He blurted out that he had had an argument over the sheep range and the other party had just blasted him in the chest. They took him to the doctor who removed the bullet, and Bob recovered fast, since he was a rugged man.

Things like this frequently happened over range pasturing during this time of new settlers in Montana. This incident was soon forgotten, though, for there were other problems that had to be met and solved every day on the range. Men did not have time to hold grudges.

When the Scotts first reached Fort Benton, Mrs. Scott insisted on walking behind the wagon. She wasn't going to take any chance of its tipping over. However, she soon became used to taking chances and the hardships one had to endure on those long trails. She came to take them in stride with the best of them and it was sure good that she did, because the Scotts had things plenty tough for a while. However, like most people of that time they toughed it through and became quite well-off.

Bob Scott, like many other men, thought there was gold in them hills, and when the gold bug bites it's hard to cure. So the whole family (that is, all except Mrs. Scott) moved to Lone Tree Park, which was between Stanford and Niehart, and a long way from any town, but a very beautiful place with lovely crags, tall trees, lots of game, and many springs.

They took along a team of horses and a few sheep, and they built a one-room cabin with an attic. The floor of the attic, where the children slept, was of split poles. One evening, after the children had been put to bed, the men were sitting by the fire smoking and talking. Bob sat there puffing on his pipe, when suddenly he said to Jack, "Do you know what day tomorrow is?"

"Why yes, tomorrow is Christmas. What can we do for those kids upstairs?"

They didn't know they had a very attentive audience in the attic, listening through the split poles with very big ears.

Jack continued, "Well, let's see. can't we make some of those dolls like we used to? You can make some jumpin' jacks you do so well. An' Batie, you make some taffy. Dave, you string popcorn an' get one of those big fir trees growing out in the back an' put it there by the gun rack."

The men made dolls and whittled jumping jacks till far into the night. Bob finally said, "Here's the dolls, but what will I use for hair? They just don't look right without some hair."

Dave, being a kid, had an idea. "Pop, I can go out to the corral an' get some wool off a sheep. That'll make good hair."

The next morning the children came down the ladder and were very surprised and impressed by the beauty and wonder of the toys under the big fir tree. It was many years before Mr. Scott knew they had lain awake upstairs during the preparations for this Christmas in the Lone Tree Park cabin. But the fact that they weren't actually surprised didn't lessen their pleasure over the beautiful tree all decorated with popcorn and bunches of green Oregon grape leaves and snowberry clusters, and they were delighted with the dolls and jumping jacks and the two sleds made from two clean grocery boxes.

The men sat back and smoked while the children played with their toys. The men were kind of proud of their handi-work and happy that the kids were enjoying the toys so much. They all stood around the Christmas tree and sang Christmas carols and Mr. Batie told the Christmas story, while over all hung the aroma of the freshly cut fir tree. Then finally Mr. Scott called them all to dinner of venison, mashed potatoes, service berries, and biscuits with wild honey. This was really a dinner. Lone Tree Park, way out in the Little Belt Mountains, south-west of Stanford, had had its first Christmas celebration.

TRIALS OF A HOBO

My definition of a hobo is a transient or migratory worker or, just as often as not, somebody who wants to see the other side of the mountains.

Angus McDonald and I decided to team up and go to Argentina; that is, we made up our minds to be hobos. Swift & Company and other meat packing companies had ranches down there and were calling for cowboys, or *gauchos* as they were called in Argentina. Mack and I had both pioneerd in Montana —punched cattle, ranched, etc.—so we thought we were pretty well-equipped for a job offered down in South America. We were well-equipped so far as knowledge went, but our finances were another thing. The most we could dig up was seven dollars apiece, but we had a dandy supply of confidence in our ability to make enough money to make the trip south.

Mack wasn't as tight with his money as the proverbial Scotsman; he had good common sense and he was a square-shooter. He was the only Scotsman I ever knew who liked snuff. The stronger it was the better it suited him.

I straightened things up on my homestead and proved up on the land, getting full title from Uncle Sam. Immediately afterward, the tall, wiry Scotsman and I went to Great Falls. A bad storm had hit near the summit of the Rockies, west of Browning, and we heard about a train on the Great Northern Railroad being stalled there, so Mack and I shipped out to shovel snow. When we arrived there, we found snow two-feet deep, and it was really cold for so early in the season. Those old flats west of Shelby Junction were one big glare of white—a white wilderness. The railroad didn't have the heavy equipment to move the snow, so it meant plenty of muscle, a No. 2 shovel, and a little courage. Snowslides can be plenty dangerous, for shovelers sometimes got caught and never got out alive. A sharp wind accompanied by below-zero temperature always made things worse.

The snowbound passengers on that train were sure glad to see us shovelers come in. They seemed to regard us as heroes, but we had no time to pose as such, for we had a big problem on our hands. The boss ordered the crew to get out and help us, and they pitched in willingly enough until that cold snow got into their shoes and the wind-driven snow hit their faces. Then they just folded up, discovering that boots, mittens, and caps with ear-muffs were a must. Working on this cold run they should have brought such things along, and I wondered why the railroad company didn't insist on them having suitable clothing before they started on a run that took them through the cold parts of Montana. However, the work train did carry a commissary car with wearing apparel in it.

Mack and I had plenty of warm clothing and were prepared for the climate. Most of the snow shovelers were members of the I.W.W.—wobblies, they were sometimes dubbed. When they first hit the snow, their leader said, "Mr. Boss, how about some heavy footgear and wool socks, caps, and mittens?"

The boss got tough and answered, "Not 'til you fellows earn them, if I have my way!"

The men folded their arms, retired to the bunk car, and started a poker game. It looked for a while as if we'd better get ready for trouble. I wondered if the railroad company might declare, "No work, no eat." This would have made things pretty serious, because the crews would have eaten anyway and this would cause fighting.

During this time, Mack and I learned a lot about the I.W.W. (Industrial Workers of the World), a new labor organization that had a big program mapped out for when the workers could claim the world. Mack and I didn't take much stock in the program, because in cow camps we'd been used to dealing man to man, fighting it out when an argument didn't settle anything. We couldn't understand how the I.W.W. could ever expect the employers to meet their demands for an eight-hour day and better working conditions. It looked to us as if they expected the millenium.

We spent most of that first day on the Great Northern doing nothing much but horsing around and eating. We slept in the bunk car that night, going to sleep wondering how things would turn out for the workers. We found out the next morning. The boss acted like a different man. He held a council with the crew leaders in the office car. They came out of the car soon afterward and announced (that is, the boss did), "Well, you fellows win. I just got a message from our Uncle Jim in St. Paul (James Hill, the railroad president). He says you get the clothes, but I hope you fellows play fair an' help us dig out. You got us by the hair an' we have to give in so we can get the cars an' passengers out of here."

They did play fair and Mack and I helped them dig out the train. After we finished we caught the first train to Columbia Falls, and then on to Kalispell. We took in the sights in Kalispell and then landed jobs as loggers in a camp owned by Hunt and Trippet of Columbia Falls. I must confess we didn't know much about logging. Instead of using the tools we'd been used to—saddle, horse, rope, and branding iron—we had to learn about logs, brush, bosses, lumber camps, and cooks. We now had to use a team, peavy, and an axe. Our wages were fifty dollars a month and chuck.

Mack was a "skidder" and I was a "swamper." This was really some change for us! Mr. Trippet had a sawmill and he cut some of the timber with his own crew. We were first taken to a kind of makeshift camp, north of Belton on the bank of Lake McDonald, a beautiful spot. This part of the country became later Glacier National Park. The scenery was grand, the snow deep, the weather cold, and there was lots of brush.

Being from the prairie, I didn't know what brush combined with deep snow could mean in a logging camp. I did soon enough, I'll tell you! It meant every time you hit a tree with

an axe, a small avalanche of snow struck you, going down
your neck, and every piece of clothing you had on got soaking
wet. A logging camp with fifty pairs of socks hung up to dry—
you never forget the perfume! I liked the place in spite of the
inconveniences. The boys were plenty rough and tough, but
they were a sociable lot and easy to get along with.

Brush means lots of hard work and planning for the swamp-
ers, because they have to cut a clear trail through the brush
for the skidders. Mack and I skidded and swamped for several
days. Come Sunday I washed my clothes along with the other
fellows. Afterward I went out exploring and sketched a few
rugged mountain scenes touched with the background of the
glaciers and the lake. There was a divine reflection of the mountains, trees, and bushes in Lake McDonald, and I tried to catch
the glory of it with my scant knowledge of painting. I knew
Charley Russell, the cowboy artist, had a cabin here somewhere,
and I looked around for it. I wasn't disappointed; Charley sure
knew a pretty place when he saw it. He called his layout Bull
Head Lodge.

We got a new cook and the boys didn't like him. He made
the mistake of trying to argue with them instead of joking. The
boys liked canned milk, which they used straight out of the
can, and they told cook that was the way they wanted it. But
cook insisted on watering the milk and serving it in a pitcher.
Then he boasted, "I know how to handle these lumberjacks,"
but he was wrong.

Monday it rained all day, so we stayed inside the cabin.
There was a lot of grumbling about a lot of things. The
wobblies among us thought they knew how to better conditions.
Some of them were "stake-bound" lumberjacks, meaning nothing would suit them until they were broke and hungry. Right
now they were saying the sugar was too sweet, the salt was
too salty, the cook no good, the boss a dictator, the hours too
long, and so on and on. In short, everything was wrong.

Some of the boys started two blackjack games. I stood by
and watched for a while and it looked so easy that I got into

one of the games. Lady Luck is fickle, let me tell you, but she sure done me right this time. I got the deal and won consistently. Two of the boys were doubling up, or playing "progressive." They doubled the bet every time they lost. A man can win or lose fast this way, and if lucky, the dealer wins pretty quickly. I soon had those bozos broke and one by one they pulled out of the game, growling and sore all over. It just seemed I couldn't lose. When the games broke up I had most of the men's money. I heard whispers all around me about red sweaters and crooks. I was wearing a red sweater, and all of a sudden it got plenty warm. Mack came up to me and said real low, "Let's keep close together, back to back—if they start anything I'll help you."

I nodded knowingly, realizing that in Mack I had a good pal. But with my pockets bulging with the boys' money, I knew anything could happen to me and Mack. I compared the situation with similar ones in the cow camps. There, no matter who won, the cowboys always laughed and said, "Well, what's the difference if I did lose, nobody dragged me into the game." Cowboys were good sports, and so were some of the boys in this outfit, but there were others who were plenty rough. This was a ticklish position to be in and I didn't feel any too comfortable as I got ready to roll up in my blanket that night.

South America on seven dollars? That's what Mack and I had to start with, but now it was different! We could travel in style to Spokane, then on to California, and finally board a ship for South America. These were my thoughts as we got settled in our bunks. That night I slept in the top bunk with Mack in front of me and a board wall at my back, with three hundred dollars in my pillow and a Colt .45 handy. I woke up when one of the men got out of his bunk and stumbled over a bench in the dark, but nothing else happened that night.

The next morning the men called a strike. We had breakfast as usual, and afterward we rolled up our blankets and started a four-mile walk to Belton, through brush and timber most of the way. Mack whispered in my ear shortly after we started, "Let me go in front of you, and keep close to me—don't take your hand off your shooting iron!" I took Mack's precaution and didn't take my hand off my gun all the way into Belton.

Belton was completely surrounded by woods, with a general store, a post office and, of course, a saloon. Mack and I got into the station and bought tickets for Spokane. We found we had three hours to wait for the train, so we went over to the saloon and looked things over and got into a poker game. Believe it or not, that red sweater of mine still seemed to bring me luck. We played for a while at the saloon; in fact, for quite a while, with me winning all the time.

We went back to the station; there was another game in progress there on a blanket on the floor, and I won some more money. One of the boys who had lost a considerable sum said, "Give us another chance to get our money back." Another piped up, "Or are you afraid?"

I couldn't pass a dare like that, so I said, "Okey, cut for the deal and name your limit." We played till the train whistled in.

I had been winning steadily, but I got up and said, "Boys, grab your money, I don't need it. The game is over."

How they scrambled! I guess they had plenty of good thoughts about me after that, and I wanted to leave them friendly.

Let me repeat again, though—gambling never pays; you win one time and you lose plenty of other times. I got so I thought life itself was gamble enough, and I quit cold on the other kind.

Mack and I arrived in Spokane at night. Mack was tired, so he went to the Great Northern Hotel right away and rented himself a room. I should have done likewise, but, outside of Chicago, this was the biggest city I'd ever been in, and I wanted to see the sights. When I was in Chicago I didn't see much because I was working for an outfit and my time there was taken up with the job.

I decided I was going to see Spokane's night life while I was there. I went to the Coeur d'Alene and to the Comique, a beer hall which is now a sedate hotel. I enjoyed the gaiety in a big casino where games were going on and money was being won and lost; the crowds were thick and the lights bright.

Finally I got pretty tired and decided to look for a bed. I couldn't locate one. There didn't seem to be any vacancies anywhere. I didn't know what to do. I walked over to a man leaning against a light pole and asked him if he knew where I could find lodgings for the night. He replied, "You can have this ticket. It's good for a ten-cent flop at the Cleveland Hotel!" I learned about cheap flophouses that night, I can tell you!

A hand under my pillow in the middle of the night woke me up. I made a grab for the hand but missed it. I felt under my pillow and discovered my roll of bills was still intact. I didn't sleep much more that night, but I figured I was lucky to still have my money. Pretty soon I didn't feel so lucky, for I found I was "crummed," or lousy. I went to work immediately and cleaned them out fast. Time is of the essence in such cases, for those skippers raise big families fast.

Mack and I got together for breakfast and exchanged experiences. While he was supposed to be sleeping peacefully, a couple of drunks in a nearby room kept him awake all night. We decided our introduction to Spokane hadn't been too cordial, yet we would stay a few days anyway. We looked around to see if we could find a job.

Spokane was a lively place: lumberjacks, railroad construction laborers, ranch hands, and miners were constantly coming and going. Everybody was optimistic and sure of himself. There wese prospectors going into the hills to find their fortunes, and land-seekers carrying blanket rolls so big they hid the men carrying them—you had to get in front to see if it was man or mule.

The wobblies didn't approve of blanket-carrying and had made a big protest about it. They maintained employers should supply blankets for their men. It finally came to that, after a lot of wrangling and threats and broken heads.

In those days there were many employment offices in Spokane, one on nearly every corner and sometimes several in between in certain sections of the city. This led to troubles because the offices were usually poorly managed and some plain dishonest. Some agencies would collect a big fee and ship men so far away they couldn't get back; others split fees with the boss on the jobs and workers would be fired fast so the agent and the bosses could get more fees from a fresh batch of workers. In fact, the standing joke was, "So-and-so has three crews—one coming, one going, and one working." This led to considerable trouble. The railroads were building west, branching out in all directions, and it took a lot of men to move the dirt with only men and horsepower. The No. 2 shovel, two horse slips, and a few "wheelers" were about all the equipment to be had, but most of the country's railroads were built with this equipment.

Mack and I got jobs in a logging camp near Bayview, Idaho. This was a bad place to work, with poor grub, low cabins, and a rough, tough boss who would kick the bunkhouse door open and yell, "All out!" And how the men did get out, since he fired any man who showed signs of common sense. Also, he never knew when it was quitting time. To top off the bad working conditions, Mack and I both got lousy; so we went back to Spokane and cleaned up, and again we took in the sights. When a man has been in the woods for a month, I'll tell you the city looks mighty nice!

The wobblies were having some trouble with the city government. They wanted to speak to the crowds on the street to organize the "jacks" and the construction laborers into "one big union," to get an eight-hour day and abolish the employment sharks. Mack and I didn't stay to see the fun. He got a teamster job and I got a swamper job near Clarkia, Idaho. We did pretty well there, since there was good timber and a nice crew in that camp. The boss was a good guy. He not only knew his work but he also knew how to handle men and get along with them.

Fishing was really good up there in the woods. Little streams were just full of fish, and the trees were majestically tall and straight, plenty of white pine and other good timber. I used to stand and admire everything around me in that beautiful, lonely wilderness: the water trickling over moss-covered mica-filled rocks, the graceful ferns, and colorful flowers. I'd wonder what secrets those tall, kingly-looking trees could tell if they could only talk; with their eight hundred years of life behind them they must have gathered plenty of secrets. They had a lovely, almost inspiring place where they had set down their roots. I, a humble being, felt like begging their forgiveness for disturbing and destroying them.

We had worked with this logging outfit for several weeks when Mack suggested that we move on again, and of course when one quit, the other would also. That was our agreement; we were true pards.

We took in the lumberjack town of St. Maries, Idaho, and found it interesting. Then we returned to Spokane, to lively doings and bright lights. We heard the "sky pilots" preach on Stevens and Washington Streets; also, there was the Salvation Army, Volunteers of America, Sister Bilkiss, Swede Shorty, the wobblies, and other groups out on the streets, all trying to sing or preach at once, and each thinking it had the only road to salvation.

I thought sadly of the old peaceful days on the range. It seems the more people you have around, the thicker get the problems. For instance, the wobblies were sure they had the answer to problems. The other side—the Chamber of Commerce, for example—were just as sure they had all the answers. I knew somebody was bound to get hurt, and in time both sides did.

Mack said one day, as we were talking the situation over, "Let's go to Hooper, Washington, and help build the new S.P.S. Railroad." I agreed, since there wasn't anything around Spokane but trouble; so we shipped out the next day, Mack as a laborer and I as a cook's flunkey. These jobs paid forty dollars a month and board for each of us. We did pretty well there. It was a dry-looking part of the country, yet there was good grass on the rolling hills. The town of Hooper and forty square miles around it belonged to McGregor Brothers, a sheep company. I still had my prejudices against sheep, so we only stuck on this job about a month, just long enough to get our traveling stake.

We left Hooper and started to beat our way to Portland, but we got ditched at Dalles, Oregon. The brakeman found us and demanded a dollar and a half. We wouldn't pay the fee and the brakeman yelled, "You guys unload or we'll unload you! She's slowing down, get off!" We needed no second command. I slid out the door of the freight car and jumped in the direction the train was moving, rolled over a few times on the ground, and busted a few cinders, but Mack landed on his feet, running fast.

The scenery was beautiful along the track by the Columbia River, but it wasn't long before Mack said, "Guess my stomach thinks my throat is cut; it's rubbing my backbone." We were both darn hungry, and something had to be done about it.

We were walking toward a farmhouse to see if we could get something to eat when I spied a big ugly dog. He didn't seem to be hankering to make our acquaintance, so we wheeled fast and hurried down the dusty road. I thought the dog looked disappointed, as though he felt he was entitled to at least one bite.

We walked along the road for a short time and soon came to an abandoned orchard. It looked like the Garden of Eden to us. The apples tasted fine. We ate quite a few and learned more about apples than we'd ever known before; they are not too good on an empty stomach. Enough said!

A slow-going "rattler" came up and we grabbed a ride and landed in Portland. We weren't expecting any reception committee, but a couple of railroad bulls seemed quite interested in us. I'd never seen a Scotsman run before but Mack did that night, almost keeping up with me. After our footrace, we found ourselves near skid row and got us a big feed. Then we went to a saloon called Erikson's. It had three big bars, really a large place.

Shortly after we arrived in Portland it started to rain, and we were told it would rain until spring. Someone told us you could tell the natives of Portland by their webfeet. Mack immediately said, "I don't want to get webfeet, how about you, Shorty?"

"Having webfeet is better than getting a crimp in the pocketbook. I'm staying right here to get another traveling stake."

Mack scowled. "Sorry, Shorty, I can't see it. It's been nice with you, but it's me for Californey."

I never saw Mack again. I landed a job as flunkey inside, where I could keep dry. I went down the Columbia River to Eufaula to work in a logging camp for the Eastern & Western Lumber Co. of Portland. It was a big company and they had good camps and a logging railroad of their own. They used donkey engines to skid logs, logs so big they cut deep ditches. I thought they were irrigation ditches till I learned better.

There were towering giant trees and big green ferns everywhere. It wasn't long before I had that hemmed-in feeling, for all I could see of the outside was now and then a small patch of sky overhead. I longed for the prairie with its blue mountains in the distance, but South America was calling, so I stayed in the Eufaula logging camp only about four weeks.

During the Christmas holidays the lumberjacks went into Portland and were not supposed to return until the New Year, but one by one they straggled back into camp, broke! The camp cook was furious because he thought he would have it easy for at least a week. The returning men were hard-working lumberjacks, but when they got into town they just couldn't control their longing for liquor. It was too bad such husky fellows couldn't manage their lives better. I finally said goodbye to the whole crowd in camp, wondering if I'd ever see any of them again.

TRAVELING ON

I WENT to Astoria and caught the steamship *Roanoke* bound for San Francisco. I signed on as a steerage passenger, but I soon changed to first-class. Steerage was terrible, full of all sorts of human beings, some of them none too clean.

The ship left dock on a day the wind was beginning to blow hard, and I looked forward to being in a real brisk storm. The sailors soon began casting lead on both sides of the ship, calling out fathoms; it was shorter by the minute. Suddenly the old captain shouted an order through his tube; the ship slowly turned about and made its way back to the Astoria dock, where she was tied up. We passengers stayed on board and told stories, some wild, and I gave out with my best yarns about Montana.

A poker game was going on in the smoking room, but I stayed out of it; watching was exciting enough. A Chinese, a Japanese, and two Mexicans were playing a tense game. Maybe if the other three could have controlled their faces like the Chinese did, they would have won some money. His expression was blank, showing no emotion whatsoever. He didn't blink an eye when he called the other fellow's bluff or got called himself.

The next morning the water was still rough, but not as rough as the night before, so we went over the bar. I was standing near midship from where I could see the ship's stern against the skyline, steadily pitching and rolling. It wasn't long before I felt like spitting, then suddenly I started "feeding" the fishes. Sheepishly, I glanced about and saw that others were doing the same thing. I soon found out that seasickness is different from any other kind of sickness. I couldn't tolerate the smell of food; in fact, I didn't much care whether I lived or died. I was like the seasick fellow who, when asked if he thought the boat was about to sink, just wailed, "Hell, I'm afraid it won't!"

Two days later we put into Eureka, California, and I was mighty glad to set my feet on shore. I still felt sick and had my "sea legs" even on land, as if I were rolling with the boat. A few hours later we sailed off again, and I didn't get seasick this time. I really enjoyed standing on the deck now and watching the changing colors of the mighty waves, and the seagulls flying playfully over the ship. We ran into a school of porpoises that leaped in and out of the water, their white bellies glistening in the sunshine. The air was salt-tinged and I was feeling first-rate; living was wonderful again.

We woke up on the fifth day to find out we were about to pass through the Golden Gate. We had been told we couldn't go ashore till daylight because San Francisco was still in ruins from its terrible earthquake and fire. We heard that thugs were running about the city, unmarked holes everywhere and basements full of water. Food was scarce and could be purchased in only a few places, and there were still fewer lodging houses.

We finally did go ashore and, believe me, we saw a sad sight—destruction everywhere. It reminded me of the biblical story of Sodom and Gomorrah. Market Street was about the only place that had been cleared of some of the debris—a space only wide enough to expose one streetcar track.

I went to the post office general delivery window, inquired for mail, and was handed a letter from Ethel C. Pomeroy, who lived in Hartford, Connecticut. I liked Ethel pretty well. She was tall and fair and she played the piano beautifully; but of course I still thought a lot of Ollie back in Montana. Ollie had so many beaus back in Montana I guess she didn't have time to write to me, but still I was discouraged because I didn't hear from her. Hearing from Ethel made me feel that anyhow one girl cared enough for me to write.

A few of the passengers from the boat went over to what was left of the Ferry Building, the depot where the boats on the bay discharged their cargo of travelers and goods. I went /

along, I'm sorry to say, for this was where confidence men, pickpockets, and others of their kind hung around. I guess I looked just right for the picking.

A nice looking young man came up to me and said, "Anybody here want a room? Good rooms, for two-fifty and up."

Knowing how hard rooms were to come by in this afflicted city, and thinking he was a hotel runner, I quickly answered, "Sure, I do."

He took me by the arm and we went a few yards to where a horse was hitched to a light wagon. He threw my baggage in back and we got on the front seat and drove off, going only a few blocks when he stopped the wagon and announced, "Here's the place." I looked around but didn't see anything that looked like a hotel or lodging house. Just then a hard-looking character with a bulldog mug came up and started to take out my baggage. I leaped to the ground and snapped. "Fellow, I'm used to carrying my own baggage."

The big bruiser looked at me and growled, "Not so fast, you owe us three dollars and fifty cents for transportation."

I gave the two of them the once-over and got a vision of picking myself up in pieces, so I forked over the money and marched off with my belongings. I considered myself plenty lucky to have got by with only the price of transportation. If I had my old Colt .45 then it would have taken a lot of self-restraint not to have used it on those crooks.

I strolled up to Van Ness Avenue where buildings were still standing and people looked real decent. The sight was still very depressing with all the tumbled-down brick and tangled steel, the ashes and blackened walls, the melted glass, and yawning holes full of water.

I later saw the fire-gutted San Francisco *Call* building, just a skeleton, and decided that with all this calamity the city had suffered it would never amount to anything again. People would move out and the place would die like some feeble old man. How wrong I was!

I went across the bay and took a steamer to Stockton, a fine

little city with many different types of people: Italians, Spaniards, Mexicans, Portuguese. The customs here were very different than in other parts of the country. For instance, in
restaurants where I had come from, the usual question was,
"Tea or coffee?"; here it was, "Wine, what kind?"

I wasn't broke, but I knew it would take quite a lot of money
to get to Argentina, so I didn't refuse the chance of a job when
an old fellow came up to me and asked, "Do you know anything about sheep?"

I answered him quickly, "Yes I do, mister." He immediately
told me, "We're lambing soon. If you're interested an' are good
help, the job pays forty a month an' board."

I went out to the hills of the coast range southeast of Stockton, to a camp near Carnegie. The camp consisted of just a
shack or two, open corrals, and poor water, but the scenery
was beautiful—rolling green hills with patches of yellow pop-
pies and plenty of live oak trees. It was February and, strangely
enough, I missed the old Montana snowbanks. The air here
seemed too heavy and close at times. I suppose I was affected
by the low altitude.

I worked here for a month, but as I look back now, I wonder
how I stood it. I had to work all day, then a night shift every
other night; the boss told me this was the California custom.

The worst-looking character I'd ever seen was the cook in
this camp. He was really something, a saloon bum, part-
Mexican, and about all he ever cooked was red beans, or
frijoles. He cooked them, rocks and all, unwashed, just as they
came from the sack. He had a little corncob pipe always hanging from his thick-lipped mouth, and drops of slobber ran off
the end when he was cooking and splashed merrily into the
gooey mess. We got plenty of pickled beef, or "red horse" as
we called it, since there was so much saltpeter used in curing it
that it made it red. No doubt cook had shaved some time in
the past, but now he had grown just plain careless and his long
whiskers were matted with filth. He never took a bath; at least
that was what I concluded from the very noticeable smell if one

went near him. When the last woolie was born I resigned. I
had definitely had enough of this place.

I traveled on to San Jose, a picturesque old town with its
palm trees waving gently in the breeze. I wondered what the
boys in Montana would say if they could have seen me basking
in the hot sunshine under palm trees, but I sighed plenty when
I thought about them and their good cooks, tasty chuck, and
fine horses.

I met a man in the hotel lobby and we had quite a talk.
He'd just returned from South America and he strongly advised
me, "Don't go down there. It's not so rosy as you think; the
big land companies charge for everything till those *gauchos*
don't have anything left, not one cent, after they get through
with you. You can't buy land cheap either, if you want to go
into business for yourself. My advice would be to go up to
Canada, where land is free and they speak your language."

I didn't like to hear such criticism of South America, land
of my dreams, but it did set me to thinking.

I worked at various jobs near San Jose until spring. One
interesting place was at Tracy, where I worked for a contractor
who planted and pruned grapevines. When I first hired out to
him, he gave me a fatherly talk which ended with, "I get along
fine with men. I never ask them to do more than I can do
myself." Believe me, I wondered afterward if he hadn't been
laughing inside when he said that.

We were digging grapevine holes, paid for by contract, the
more holes dug the more *he* got, not us! We tried to keep up
with his digging, but none of us could. I used to get so tired
I couldn't eat any supper. Then I discovered the big pitcher
on the table contained wine; after that I took a good drink of
wine at suppertime and I found eating wasn't so difficult.

The owner of the vineyard next to the one where I was
working was an Italian, and he induced me and two others to
quit and come and work for him. He and his family were nice
people. They treated us square, but a little too free with the

wine. Claret—dago red, some called it—was the wine they served most; it was simply clarified, fermented grape juice.

Some of the men told me this country gets dry and burnt up in the summer, but as it looked so nice in late winter and spring I wasn't certain they were telling the truth. A long time later I came to believe them.

I met a little Italian girl, Vegi. She was very pretty and we had some good times together. She could sing like a lark, which made her even more attractive to me for I always liked music. I didn't have any serious intentions because girls would interfere with my plans to go to Argentina. Then I met another fellow who told me to stay away from South America; he emphatically declared that the good old U.S.A. was the best place in the world.

I had my fill of vineyard work so I went to San Francisco and boarded the S.S. *Umatilla* for Seattle. It was a nice six-day trip and this time I didn't get seasick. One whole family had to stay in bed all the time of passage. An old sea-dog on board told me, "If you don't hanker to feed the fish, jes' chew terbacker." He must have followed his own advice for his chin was bobbing up and down all the time.

We landed in Seattle in the middle of fog and rain, but I liked the looks of the waterfront. It was a lively place, with the big ships from foreign countries standing by, their crews talking in their own strange languages.

I got a job on a dairy ranch at Cedar River, south of Renton. The owners were nice people and they had good cattle. We shipped milk to Seattle every morning. One morning when I went to get the team to take the milk to the station, I couldn't find them anywhere. Finally I located them inside the stump of a mammoth old cedar. They were just lying down there, resting peacefully. Trees grow plenty big in this country.

I got itchy feet again, though I had decided not to go to Argentina just yet, anyway not before seeing British Columbia and Alberta. I traveled by boat up to Victoria, a beautiful city. I received another letter from Ethel Pomeroy while in Victoria.

I also received a letter from Montana telling me Ollie Scott had married Marvin Drinkard, a schoolteacher from Lewistown. I was stunned for a while; I thought about getting married myself, just for spite. Of course I wasn't ready for marriage yet and came to my senses before I did anything too irrational. As a matter of fact, I was scared of marriage, but the news of Ollie's marriage kind of broke me up.

Within a few days I traveled eastward over the mountains, past great jagged snow-capped peaks, past moving glaciers. I saw forest-clad slopes cut here and there by deep gorges through which clear, pure streams poured on their way to the sea. The keen air sent a feeling of hope through me, and a wave of energy.

I saw many scenic spots and plenty of wild terrain in British Columbia. There were rich mines and good timber; hunting and fishing were wonderful. I went through Ferny, a tent city, for it had just been burned down by a great forest fire, but it was bravely rising from its ashes; in fact, it looked so new that it reminded me of Montana in the old days.

I passed through Frank, where a big mountain had suddenly split and slid down over a large part of the town, burying many people; then on to Lethbridge, Alberta, a coal mining town. Here they also had cattle, and they raised hay to feed the cattle. I went on to Edmonton, where I talked with people about the Peace River country. I was told the soil froze up, there was no transportation, and that it was a long ways from the markets, so I didn't go up there, but many times since I wished that I had.

I traveled to Lacomb, Alberta, then west to Medicine Valley, and here I took up a homestead. Later, I found that it wasn't very productive land. The soil looked fine, but the frost got too heavy for one to be able to do much with the land. Most of the good land plots had been taken by the Hudson Bay Co. or the schools. I soon decided not to give up my precious U.S. citizenship, but I did stay here a while, working as a hod carrier for builders all summer.

I received another letter from Ethel, a sweet one. I hoped she would keep on writing to me. It was good to have a friend like Ethel, even though I didn't want to be led to the altar yet.

I left Canada and found myself again back in Spokane, the pleasant city among the pines and waterfalls. I stayed in and around here until the fall of 1909. They were having a pretty lively time with the wobblies, and during the fall and winter months the free-speech and other various fights and strikes were going full tilt. It meant busted heads and jail for many men. The wobblies demanded the use of the streets for their forums, as other organizations did, but the police department told them, "nothing doing." John Sullivan, chief of police, was considered a pretty tough guy to deal with, so the scene was set for considerable action and excitement.

The wobblies claimed they were *the* labor union and they tried to reach the many transients working in the railroad company construction camps, the logging camps, and mines. The wobblies were out for free speech, abolishment of employment offices, and an eight-hour day for all workers; in short, it was the aim of the wobblies to abolish capitalism and run the show with labor. It seemed a simple thing to do, but it wasn't, as they soon found out. Each time a wobblie began to speak his piece on the street an officer of the law would come along and slam him in jail.

The wobblies came up with another plan—fill the jails to overflowing and make it too expensive for the authorities to continue the fight! The wobblies sent out a call for volunteers to come to Spokane to speak on the streets, and did they come! They came by the hundreds until they filled the city jail, the county jail, the abandoned Franklin school. There were tales of violence and brutal beatings to be heard every day.

They sent East for an organizer. Elizabeth Gurley Flynn, a young woman just out of school, arrived and became the wobbly queen. She had great influence with all the boys, maybe because she was so pretty and also so smart. I hold no brief for her actions, good or bad, but her arrest resulted in some kind of draw and she was let go free and, I am thankful to say, nobody got hung. Her case lasted all summer and was finally thrown out of court.

I heard that the prisoners in the Franklin school were starved and beaten unmercifully. Wobblies called this place "Spokane's bull pen." Sister Belkiss, self-styled evangelist, wrapped herself in the American flag and went out to speak on the streets with the Bible in her hand and a photographer with her. She, too, was arrested, and shortly after her arrest Police Chief John Sullivan was shot and killed. His killer was never found.

One day hell broke loose on Stevens and Washington Streets; the wobblies made a raid on the employment offices, beat up the men who ran them, smashed windows and furniture, and threw the furniture and men into the streets. I remember seeing a signboard in the river near the Great Northern depot. The sign had the name ADAMS & SWITZNER, LABOR AGENCY painted on it and was being carried merrily down the stream by the bobbing waves. I saw many labor agents racing madly down the street with the wobblies in close pursuit. If their looks meant anything, I can tell you the wobblies sure didn't mean to tell those agents how much they loved them!

I left Spokane soon after this little ruckus and went to a job near Sandpoint, Idaho. It was back to the woods for me. I watched the stories in the paper about the trouble in Spokane and soon read that the trouble was over and everybody was loving everybody else. The wobblies had gained the right to speak in the streets upon obtaining a permit from the city. They later got the eight-hour day, and some of the camps put in baths and clean bedding.

I worked all summer in and around Spokane. I was in the U.S. fire camps some of the time. Uncle Sam furnished us with Swift's premium ham and the best of other chuck, and paid good wages. There was a lot of danger on this job, and in some localities we faced the "widow-maker" several times. It gets pretty frightening sometimes when flames are roaring at you from the treetops and traveling fast. It's all right if there's a

place to get away from the fire and you have time to get protection from the fiery inferno. Most fire bosses had such things
figured out and were trusted by their men.

Luck was with me. I was out of this work before the big
fire of 1910 that swept away so much of that marvelous growth
of timber, and in which a great number of lives were lost. There
were many stories of heroism to be heard afterward. The nation
lost a great heritage, for many of the destroyed trees were a
a thousand or more years old. People should think twice before
carelessly tossing away a hot match or a lighted cigarette in a
wooded area. We as a nation are so rich in natural resources
I fear we do not realize that everything except space has a
limit, and now some scientists claim even that has a limit.

I have worked in so many logging camps, mills, and fire
crews that I may have seen the picture of mass destruction of
our forests a little clearer than most people. I loved those tall
whispering trees and their primitive setting in those beautiful
mountains where the water cascades down over mossy stones
among the ferns, flowers, and bear grass. Yes, it's beautiful,
the scent of trees, the scenery, and the game in the forests.

I hate fires, but I liked the crews that fought the fires, and
the chuck was grand, as well as all the excitement. The one
thing I dislike is man's carelessness and destruction of things
nature put here for our use and welfare. Many times I have
seen what destructive logging operations can do. I myself have
had to chop down as many as forty trees to get one large tree
out to the skids. The high line used by many outfits drag down
much of the young growth, and careless burning operations
often cause fires that do great damage.

Americans, especially the people in this great West, must
learn the value of the forest, as well as appreciate the beauty
of their green heritage. Whole civilizations have disappeared
because of the destruction of forests. Without our trees we have
a quick run-off of snow water, dry streams in summer, scarce
water for power and irrigation, soil erosion and finally a *desert*.
It's up to those who love the great outdoor sports of hunting

and fishing to protect these forests that nature made for us. I
like to think of a great tree whispering:

> *Way up here in the blue sky*
> *I am great and beautiful;*
> *Can you tell me why?*
> *Take care of me and keep me*
> *Forever tall and beautiful,*
> *For future generations to see.*

I GET HITCHED

ONE DAY I received an offer of one thousand dollars for my homestead in Montana. I wrote to the prospective buyer, Otto Schott, that if he would make it twelve hundred, he could have my place. He answered that he would agree to my price since he needed good pasture badly; he owned a nice ranch south of Stockett. He had been my good friend and neighbor for a long time, and I was mighty glad to be going back to Great Falls to close the deal, and to be able to see my beloved mountains again.

Arriving at my homestead, I found that the pack rats had taken over as usual. To have a place to sleep I had to clean them out at once. I had a system for doing this; it worked sometimes: I put a pan on the edge of a cup that had some bait in it; Mr. Rat gets curious, and when he wiggles that cup the pan drops and the rat is trapped.

I discovered I also had tenants in my barn, a nice little family of skunks! I didn't want to catch them, I just wanted to get rid of them! I kept close watch and when that old lady had her little flock out for an airing, I closed the barn door tight. They took the hint and left, thank goodness! It's strange how soon wild life takes over an empty building, especially in the mountains. I never liked to have to kill helpless creatures. Animals are part of God's creation and have as much right to life as do human beings.

I visited a few of my old neighbors and then went into Stockett and closed the deal with Otto. But I felt pretty downcast when I said goodbye to majestic Old Tiger Butte.

I received another letter from Ethel Pomeroy. It set me to thinking that I was a pretty lonely fellow and maybe ought to have a real life partner. So I got up spunk enough and wrote a pretty important letter, asking Ethel if she would come to the wild and wooly West to stay for keeps. I got a quick reply— her answer was *YES* in big letters. I wondered if she had been waiting for me to pop the question all along. Well, maybe she had and maybe I'd been missing something for a long time.

Ethel came to Great Falls in September 1911, and we were married in the home of my sister, Mrs. Elizabeth Blaine. I was very proud of my beautiful blond wife with the sweet blue eyes, proud too of the way she could tame the most stubborn piano and make it speak real music. It made me feel quite set up that a girl like Ethel would give up a good job as telephone operator to hitch up with a fellow like me. I resolved never to let her regret her decision.

Ethel and I decided to go out to Idaho and make a fresh start among those lakes and tall pines. I said farewell to the Montana prairie and mountains a little reluctantly, I confess, but it seemed like the best thing to do. I bought a house and two acres in Hauser Junction. I worked in the orchards during the summer and in the woods in the winter. Ethel and I got along fine; we were happy, especially when Ethel returned from visiting her sister in Texas where our first child was born— John, a real Texan. This was in 1912 and, believe me, I was sure proud of this chunky, blue-eyed, good-natured little fellow. My first-born! I went around treading air, bragging about him to everybody who would listen.

I took a job at Newman Lake where an irrigation ditch was being dug. I left Ethel and the baby at home; she was giving piano lessons to the children of the neighborhood, making a little extra money which came in handy.

I hadn't been on the irrigation job long before the wobblies on the job pulled a strike, and I had to join them. We were asking for eight hours' work what the boss wanted to pay us for ten hours' work. The boss refused and called us all into his office. When we were lined up before his desk, he said, "It's the old wages. It's up to you, you can take it or leave the job.

I got my pen in one hand an' the checkbook in the other. Who wants to be first?"

Seemed as if all the men wanted to be first the way they crowded up to him. The wobblie leader's turn came and the boss tried to scare him, saying, "I've a good mind to poke you in the eye! You're the fellow who caused all the trouble! An' see what it got you? Your pals are acceptin' the old wage—an' they're glad to get it."

The leader grinned crookedly and snapped, "Get busy and write out my check quick! Better not start what you can't finish. Times have changed; eight hours are a day's work now. I didn't make this trouble—evolution did it. Goodbye!"

Every one of the men followed him off the premises, and I guess the boss had a lot of thinking to do. He tried to replace us, but he discovered it wasn't easy. He calmed down in a few days and asked us to come back. We did, and got the pay we'd asked for. We finished the ditch in May when the orchards needed water. Now there was plenty of water for irrigation purposes and everybody was happy.

The White Pine Sash and Door Company of Spokane set up a sawmill at Hauser Lake where lumber was sawed into shop lumber, wide boards over two inches thick. Later, as needed, it was resawed by other mills into standard size boards. My job was piling the hard-to-handle shop lumber. I was paired with Jerry Finlan of Hauser Junction. He was a big young Irishman from the "old sod," and we got along fine, but it nearly finished me to hand up those heavy planks to him. He weighed 210 and I a scant 140. Whenever I saw him spit on his hands, I knew what it meant—speed up there, Shorty.

We piled and piled until Hauser Junction looked like a real flourishing lumber yard. Then one day, like all lumber mills, it closed. The saying is: "They log out, burn out, and pull out." This was certainly the truth; they didn't last long.

I went to work for Lewis Otterson of Post Falls. He was a contractor with a lot of horses. I worked for him until September 1914, when our second son was born. I made up my mind then, since I had an increase in my family and could do no more running around, that I would have to stay put on one job. For several years we got along very well, with me working close to home.

March 1918 brought us our third son, Tommy, who was born at Hauser Junction the night Russia started her revolution. I began to think that if the boys kept on coming to our house, I'd have a full baseball team. The trend changed for us after we moved to Spokane in 1920. This time it was a girl, a pretty little bundle of joy, and we named her Florence.

Now I did have to stay on the job, but luckily we were all well and happy. I began working for the Washington Water Power Company shortly after our arrival in Spokane. We bought a cheap house and fixed it up. Then, after we had lived in it for four years, I sold it for nearly three times as much as I'd paid for it.

We Storks then did the usual thing expected of Storks: we moved back to the land, loving the land as had generations of Storks before me. This time it was eighty acres of stump land at Deer Park, Washington. I cleared and burned till I just about finished myself. My family enjoyed the place, but I didn't have time to enjoy anything. I was trying to bring that piece of land into production before we starved out on it. Finally my sister Ida helped us some, bless her! But I had to give up shortly after her help, for I got the flu and nearly passed on. I sold the place and bought another home in Spokane.

I went to work for the Union Pacific Railroad shops. Then 1925 brought tragedy to my family: my sister Bessie died and shortly after her death our son Tommy passed away with scarlet fever. The other children had it too but we saved them, thank God! We couldn't stand the house with Tommy gone, so we traded it for a house and eight acres west of the city, near what is now Geiger Field, the city's air terminal. We bought a mule team, a cow, and five hundred chickens.

We did pretty well the first year we were out there. I grew potatoes, corn, and raised chickens. I had quite a time with big rats from a nearby hog ranch; I guess the garbage fed to the hogs invited the rats, and I was plenty discouraged when those big rats killed so many of my chickens. One morning I felt like crying when I opened the brooder house and saw forty of my best chicks piled in the corner, their throats cut by those pesky rats.

My family had a lot of fun here; we had friendly neighbors and somebody was always giving a card party or dance. One Christmas I played Santa Claus for the neighborhood kids. I sure had some of them puzzled. They wondered why Santa was so full in the front and so flat in the behind. Kids are smart sometimes and hard to fool. I would like to say right now: It would be a pretty lonely old world without kids, even if they do act contrary more often than we sometimes wish.

I finally gave up fighting the rats and bought a house on North Nevada Street in Spokane, seven rooms and a $1200 debt against it. I hustled around and worked at various jobs, and eventually paid off the debt, painted the house, fenced in the yard, and had it all in good order when jobs became really scarce and I decided something had to be done.

Ethel and I saw an advertisement about a place southwest of Chewelah, Washington. We went to see it and decided it looked like a good proposition: 160 acres, a good house, eighty of the acres in alfalfa, ten head of pure-bred Jersey cows, an established milk route, and plenty of farm equipment. We traded our home for the place, going into debt again, this time to the tune of $4000.

We moved out there feeling optimistic. The milk route, which brought $150 a month, was in the hills near the magnesite quarry west of Chewelah. It was real hard work to milk twice a day, bottle and deliver the milk every morning, then plow all afternoon, or cut wood or fix fences, and do the other necessary farm jobs. I liked what I was doing, though, and that made a difference, for when a man likes a job it seems to carry him along on wings.

Our new home was in the Mountain View district and it

was known as the Old Chris King place. The location was beautiful. There was good water, plenty of trees for shade, and some dense forest. All about us were blue hills, and when we looked toward the south, we could see distant Lane's Mountain. The schoolhouse not only served for the children but was also used for dances and other entertainments. It was really "hillbilly country," everybody sociable, happy, and poor.

The finances of three families combined to purchase a second-hand binder, and we used it alternately to get our crops in for the winter. Nobody went hungry in our little settlement. Everybody helped the other person whenever help was needed. Ever so often there would be a picnic or a birthday celebration with ice cream, chicken, salads, pies, garden stuff, and plenty of fiddlin' too.

Some who raised goats made their ice cream with goat's milk. It looks whiter than cow's milk or cream, and some people don't like goat's milk, but it's supposed to be the best kind. Goats don't get tuberculosis like cows do; I guess goats are too tough to catch diseases. But we had plenty of ice cream made out of real cow's cream too.

The boys had to go to school in Chewelah, a distance of ten miles, and it was quite a trick to get them there when the snow was deep, but somehow we managed, because they had to have an education. The Hoover depression had begun, and we wondered what was going to happen. We found out, all right! The boardinghouse cut its milk order in half; the price of cream went down and down. I found sales dropping everywhere and I had milk on my hands. Men were getting laid off all around us. Most of my alfalfa had frozen out, so I had to seed grain for hay, and this meant a pile of extra work. My family helped in every way they could; everybody tried to be cheerful by being busy all the time.

There were many deer up in this high country. I suppose it could be called a deer paradise, because the hills, springs, dense brush, and tall trees were fine for these animals. I loved to watch them, such fleet-footed beauties, although they were sometimes a nuisance when they got into the planted fields.

One day John, not yet in his teens, rushed excitedly into the house. He cried, "Pop! I got a deer!" I went to look and sure enough he'd shot a deer with a .22 rifle. Quite a trick for a kid, or anybody for that matter, the way he did it—in the back, severing the spinal cord. Let the man who thinks he can shoot try that!

One morning as I was hitching the team to the sled, preparing to deliver the milk, John and I heard a commotion out in the woods. John ran to see what was going on; the howling and barking suddenly stopped as he went through the trees, and he saw coyotes and dogs slinking away as if they were ashamed of what they had done. A poor little fawn lay bleeding on the ground. John quickly put it out of its misery and left it there.

It was quite a job to locate our cows in the midst of the tangle of brush and trees. Sometimes we couldn't find them, in spite of the fact that we had bells on them. It was even difficult not to get lost ourselves in the brushy trails. My son Bob was a good hand at finding the cows, and he liked the job. I guess it was because he found it fun to ride the buckskin pony. I warned him to be careful not to touch the baby fawns in the wilderness, because a fawn with the scent of a human being on it becomes an orphan; its mother will have nothing more to do with it, won't even feed it.

That winter the deer had a tough time of it. The snow was deep up in the hills—four feet or more of settled snow, crusted on top—the deer couldn't walk on it and had to keep to the main trails. Coyotes, cougars, and dogs had easy pickings.

I cut cordwood out by the spring in our woods, and had wood corded all over the place. I sure loved to work out there, to fell the tall, dry tamarack trees which were hard to saw but easy to split, and the hardest wood I ever came across. Once in a while I ate my lunch alone by the spring where I could really get my bearings, consider the Great Architect of the grandeur surrounding me, and put myself in His hands.

I put out hay for the deer once in a while but they seemed

afraid and wouldn't eat it .They would browse on the twigs and tree moss till they caught the scent of me, then they'd throw up their heads, give a little snort, roll their big eyes, wiggle their ears, and disappear fast. Truly, the price of life for deer is eternal vigilance. Squirrels and chipmunks will chatter and run when they think there's anything foreign to their safety nearby, and the deer depend a great deal on these little neighbors of theirs who see, hear, and smell so well, for they tell about the dangers ahead.

There was a flock of Chinese pheasants out in my woods, too, and I made friends with them, getting some of them to feed quite close to me. The male—cock of the walk—would let his harem eat first while he paraded about showing them his beautiful tail feathers and fine top-knot. He would feed alone, all the time watching me. The wood I piled made nice roosting places and the pheasants used them to good advantage. Many times I saw these friendly wild fowls feeding with our chickens.

Ethel and the children enjoyed living here. She was always happiest when she was getting ready for a party or making pies and cakes for a grange picnic. I couldn't go out much at night because I had to get up so early in the morning to milk the cows, but how I did enjoy the winter evenings in our home with the fire crackling merrily in the big wood stove. We played a lot of pinochle. Bob would tease his mother about cheating. He would shuffle the cards and make her believe he thought she was cheating. We would have heaps of fun trying to prove she hadn't been cheating.

We lived near the schoolhouse and there was always something going on there; it was called the Mountain View School. Gone are the days of the grange meetings with the speeches, singing, and dances; the old schoolhouse has been abandoned. Talking about the old meetings in the schoolhouse brings to mind the old man who always insisted on singing "The Daring Young Man on the Flying Trapeze." He always wondered why the audience didn't appreciate hearing good music. Colter, the old gentleman, was a bachelor who lived a lonely life, and attending the meetings was his only chance to show off.

I was out of bed at 4 A.M., then I milked, separated the milk, and went on my delivery route to the quarry. I liked the trip; I got all the latest news about my neighbors and quite a little gossip. I would return home to be met by Ethel in her little white apron, and she would immediately ask me, "Well, what's new today?" or "Whose goose was cooked this time?"

After I ate my breakfast, I would go out to the fields or woods and get busy again. Sometimes when I saw deer in the middle of my hay meadow, carelessly trampling down what I'd worked so hard to raise. I'd get plenty sore, as if they could know they were doing wrong; but the instant they saw me they would race off, jump lightly over the fence, and make for the woods like mad.

The magnesite quarry where I delivered milk was an interesting place located in a cozy nook in the beautiful hills by Brown's Lake. It looked something like a mining town and it was the home of about two hundred people who worked there. There was no store, only a boardinghouse, but it was a nice little community with peaceful, happy people. A tramway had been built to carry quarry rock seven miles down to Chewelah where the processing was done. The Northwest Magnesite Company seemed to get on well with its help, and the company contributed a lot to the prosperity of Chewelah and the surrounding country.

Chewelah is situated in a fertile valley, with great forest-covered mountains, white cliffs, and crags on both sides. The trip to Chewelah is worthwhile for the view if nothing else. There are lakes with many fish, there is good hunting, and many varieties of colorful wild flowers. Hay, beef, and butter are shipped out of Chewelah, and it is the home of the Curlew Creamery, the creamery that coined the slogan: "It's made its way by the way it's made"—meaning their ice cream. I've always thought the sweet alfalfa, warm sunshine, and good water in that locality had much to do with the quality of that popular cold confection.

The painting urge just about overwhelmed me while I was in this picturesque part of the country, but I conquered the urge because it takes time to paint, and I didn't have the time! I soothed myself with the thought that maybe some day I would have time to paint. Right now I had a real job, a big debt to clear, the very thought of which scared me. My family had longed to live in the country and I'd thought the milk route would pay handsomely. Now I had misgivings, but I didn't say anything to the family to worry them, although I could see that cloud on the business horizon looming larger every day.

One day I got into my 1922 Overland car—Florence called it "Papa's pride and joy"—and drove to Spokane fifty miles away. As I entered the city, I saw big signboards saying: BUSINESS IS GOOD. KEEP IT GOOD. This set me to pondering real hard. Just how good is business if we have to be told it's good! I asked myself.

I returned to the ranch and was met by Ethel, asking, "I just heard that the boardinghouse was closed and won't be opened again. What does it mean, Claude, what does it mean?"

"It means we'll have to look for other customers," I replied. "But maybe the news you got is wrong, maybe someone just started a rumor."

I went to our telephone hanging on the wall and rang up some of our neighbors. One by one, they confirmed the bad tidings. The boardinghouse that had been using a lot of milk had really shut down. Now I *was* scared!

Next day I went into Chewelah again, taking a calf hide and some cream, and I found out just how good business in general was! Cream prices were way down and the best I could get for the hide was thirty-five cents. Everybody in town was talking hard times. I had to draw on our savings to buy groceries.

It began to dawn on me for sure that we were in for bad times, but I had faith in the good old U.S.A., the country that has always found a way to solve its problems. I just kept on milking, separating the cream, and selling milk at the quarry. It was really tragic the way they were laying off those men at the quarry, and of course I lost my customers one by one. I sure felt sorry for them, especially those with children to feed. Some of those people only took a pint of milk a day, and I couldn't make much profit anyway. Finally I said to Ethel, "Let's bottle the skimmed milk and give it away if those families will take it." Ethel agreed that this was a good idea and we put it to work. Most of the families were glad to get the free milk for their children. I just told them, "You'd better take it. I won't bill you for it. Probably we'll all be broke before things get better."

Winter came and I spent lots of hours cutting wood. I sent some of it to Spokane, but even wood didn't sell; there were too many people out of work. The dances in the schoolhouse continued, but I detected an uneasy expression on the faces of those stump farmers who had families to support.

My kids went to school, happy as usual, for they were not aware about material things. This is one of the advantages of childhood.

I shoveled and plowed snow until I was about ready to drop in my tracks, but I knew heavy snow made things nice and green in the summer. This year, in particular, we must grow extra good crops.

Then one day Ethel and I had a serious talk. We could stay on the farm, work ourselves to pieces, and probably lose out in the end. We were getting along in years, and making another change would be tough, but we had to do something. Decisions are hard to make sometimes and this was one of those times.

Listening to the radio the next day, I heard President Hoover say that we might have to go off the gold standard, and he condemned the "money hoarders"; he also said, "Let's save the banks." I thought, well, I haven't got a bank, but my family and I have to eat. I knew I'd better go into Spokane and get what little money I had in the bank or maybe we'd go hungry.

I knew now that we were through on this place. I had everything on the farm mortgaged except a small increase in stock. I tried to sell the six fine thoroughbred Jersey calves, but nobody seemed to have the money to pay for them. We all loved the young calves but we had to be rid of them, so I butchered them. It was just like doing murder, I thought, and poor John cried. I took our other calves to Spokane and had a hard time selling them, finally letting them go to Meecham Brothers for five cents a pound. The boss there told me I'd better take the check to the bank at once because he wouldn't guarantee how long it would be good.

Needless to say, I did just that. I also drew out the little money we had in the bank. It was lucky I did, for the bank soon closed up and it was a long time before it could pay its depositors.

On my way out of town I saw a neat-looking house on Howard Street with a sign on it that read: FOR SALE—$800. I took a look at the inside of the house and decided it would do pretty well for my family. I decided to bring Ethel in to see the house as soon as possible. I'd driven nearly to Deer Park when the thought struck me that by the time I got back with Ethel, the house might be sold. Cheap houses were being picked up fast; people didn't have money enough for the high-priced houses. I turned around and went back to Spokane and closed the deal. I paid fifty dollars down and agreed to pay twelve dollars a month until the house was paid for in full. It was a good deal and I needed that kind of break. This is one deal I've never been sorry for making.

I returned to the ranch, told Ethel what I'd done, and all seemed smooth. The kids didn't want to go back to town and they did a little grumbling, but not too much. I had McHugo Transfer Company send one of their big trucks to the farm, and we moved to Spokane. We even took Florence's cute, devilish-acting little goat. We took a gallon of cream and ten gallons of milk, so all our new neighbors had milk and cream along with us for a while. We also brought thirteen cords of the finest dry tamarack wood; we wouldn't have to worry about keeping warm for some time.

It was 1932 when we moved back to town. I hadn't had a late morning sleep for a year and a half, so it seemed like being in heaven to rest late in the morning. However, I did this for only a couple of days, for I had to go out looking for work.

I remember Ethel's niece Val was at our house the day I came in and said, "Just look at a fellow who made three dollars today!" They pretended it was a joke and laughed it off, for which I was thankful.

I had put an advertisement in the newspaper: "Good gardener—will do anything." A lady called up and said she wanted linoleum put under a bathtub without disturbing the plumbing. I had my doubts about doing the job, but I thought I'd try it. So I went ahead with the job and accomplished the feat, by myself too, for which I was very proud. This job netted me $3.50. This is the way things were for some time, a little money earned here and there, but I managed to keep things going.

The kids started school in Spokane; that is, all but John. He stayed in Chewelah and finished the semester there. I traded a horse with Mrs. Peters for his board and room. Robert and Florence got along well at Rogers High School, and finally vacation came. We put in the summer in one way and another, and I managed to keep up the payments on the house, although it wasn't easy.

Ethel was looking a little dragged-out, not even playing her beloved piano. I began to worry, and little Florence, always a helpful little miss, also seemed to be worried about her mother.

Fall came and jobs were still scarce. We heard the news over the radio that Franklin D. Roosevelt was elected President. This announcement gave us all hope and confidence, since he promised quick action. Things did begin to happen—the bank holiday, the WPA. I got a job on the WPA for a time and it sure helped our finances.

Times gradually grew better. I had my garden jobs and

even managed to save a little money. Ethel got a job as matron in the Greyhound Bus station, the first time she had worked for pay since our marriage. I was afraid the work would be too hard for her, but she laughed and said it was easy. She got fifty dollars a month and was proud of it.

Both boys graduated from high school and took positions away from home. John went to business college for a while, took a civil service examination, passed it easily, and secured a government job. Bob took up teaching and Florence graduated from high school; it now looked as though I could ease up a little, since there was only Ethel and myself to work for.

But fate stepped in again. Ethel had a stroke and a nurse had to be brought in for her care. Poor Ethel lingered on for four years, suffering all the time and gradually growing weaker. She passed away in 1943, just when life could have been smoother for us. I laid her away after thirty-two years of marriage and came home alone.

THE LOST PROSPECTOR

AFTER Ethel's passing, the house seemed very empty; yet there were so many memories. I had no regrets about our life together. Always I had done the best I could for her and our children. There was one thing I did wish, though, that I could have been able to find her father for her. . . .

One day back in 1911 when we had been married a short time, Ethel said to me, "Claude, do you know, I wish so much I could find my dad. He left Hartford for Alaska in 1900. For some years we heard from him, very interesting letters describing places and telling us things that were happening to him. Then, finally no more letters, nothing but silence. I have worried so much about it. Do you suppose we could do anything to find him?"

I had seen quite a few elderly prospectors in my time; they were all rough, tough old fellows who knew their way around. Some of them had gone up to that frozen wilderness and failed to return, so I was not surprised at Ethel's father having dropped out of sight, for he was fifty-one years old when he started out.

I told Ethel what I thought, but she said, "No, I believe Dad is still alive. He was a pretty tough man, though he did not look it. You should hear the things that happened to him." And gradually she related his story. We talked about him so much and searched so long that I came to call him Dad just as she did.

He was born in Briston, Connecticut, in 1846. His father was a precision instrument mechanic and clockmaker. As soon as Dad was old enough, he also learned the trade and became very efficient, for he was thorough in everything he did. But

118

that kind of life was too tame for him; he wanted to go West, hunt buffalo, fight Indians and, above all, look for gold.

He had heard stories of the great West, the really wild West of those days. The characters enchanted him—the trappers, the Indians, cowboys, soldiers. When he was seventeen he tried to enlist in the Union Army in the Civil War but was unsuccessful; he was slender, underweight, and not very well developed. He was, however, much tougher than he appeared, and he didn't give up. He worked his way through Union Army camps and made a few dollars, which he spent about as fast as he earned them. He wrote back to the family that while en route to St. Louis he had seen five horse thieves hanging from one big tree. That was at Quincy, Illinois, and was not an unusual sight in those days, for horse thieves were always dealt with pretty severely.

When he finally landed in St. Louis, he had just three cents. The three cents could not satisfy his hunger, so he bought a cigar with the coppers. He always liked cigars, smoked them all his life. He headed into the first business house he came to and boldly said, "Mister, I'm broke and need a job. Can you use me? I'll do anything!"

The broker, a large, prosperous-looking man, looked young John up and down and asked his experience. He finally said, "Kid, you got to get experience. I know it's tough to be broke. Tell you what, you go over to that big boardinghouse and tell them I sent you."

He got the job, general roustabout and errand boy, and since he was energetic, honest, and agreeable, he became quite popular. He liked this job though it did not pay much. His free time he spent down on the levee. Here he met the soldiers, hunters, trappers, and others who rode the steamboats up and down the Missouri, to and from the West, land of his dreams. He saw them leave, rugged plainsmen, buffalo hunters, trappers, Indian scouts, soldiers, sportily dressed gamblers, and, of course, painted ladies. On the returning boats he would see the same characters returning after time spent deep in the wilder-

ness of the Old West, often in hostile Indian country. Stories
of adventure, easy gold, Indians, and buffalo all interested him
intensely, especially those of the easy gold.

He was too adventurous and lively a youth to stand up long
under all this excitement without doing something about it.
Something seemed to be drawing him to the West, and pulling
hard too. One day the steamboat *Peora City* tied up at the dock.
It was loaded with blue-uniformed soldiers going out to put
down an Indian uprising. Dad gulped, swallowed a lump, and
said, "Now! Now is the time."

Dad immediately went into action. Approaching an officer,
one Lieutenant Donohue, he asked to be enlisted at once for
Indian fighting. The officer looked him over, laughed, and said,
"Kid, you better get back to mom, an' quick. This is a man's
job an' there's more to it than fun." Dad insisted so loudly,
and became so determined that the attention of the company
captain was attracted. He walked over to see what it was all
about. He was a rough-looking man, but he had a twinkle in
his eye. When he was told, "This kid wants to fight Indians,"
the captain said, "Is that right, kid? Did you ever get spanked?
Oh, hell, we need men, Sarge, sign him up and give him
so-and-so's equipment."

Dad could hardly believe his ears. Now he was a man, a
soldier. Not until the next day did he realized he was enlisted
and serving under a dead man's name. This was a common way
of filling vacancies at the time. There were many men in the
West then who for various reasons did not care to have their
real names mentioned. Things like this can and did lead to
complications, but Dad didn't care; he was in and going West,
that's what counted. His outfit, the 21st New York Infantry,
was a tough and boisterous one, but for all that the men were
big-hearted and generous, often to a fault, especially in cards.

Three months later the Indians were subdued after several
hard and dangerous battles, and the outfit was discharged at
Leavenworth, Kansas, where Dad had various jobs and then
went on to Kansas City. Here he worked as runner at the Gillis

Hotel for a while, and in the winters of 1865 and 1866 went through the terrible cholera and smallpox epidemics. Hundreds died and their clothes and bodies were burned in long lines up and down the water front. The things he saw here, the misery, death, and sickness, were terrible and left a deep impression on him. Strangely enough, he did not contract the disease, though he nursed a pal through it.

Kansas City was a particularly tough place at this time. One night a customer of the hotel was shot in front of the hotel. Dad ran out into the street, picked up the injured man, and carried him in and put him to bed.

The manager said, "John, get a doctor, quick!"

There was still shooting going on outside, so Dad said, "Just give me that gun there in the drawer." And out he went, got the doctor, and they saved the man from bleeding to death.

While he was out after the doctor, he saw a bunch grab a Chinese man and make the poor fellow sing in Chinese and dance while they shot at his feet. It's queer what some people call entertainment, especially when they've had a few drinks.

Dad got itchy feet again and had to travel, ever westward. So on July 15, 1867, he enlisted in Company C, 18th Kansas Cavalry. Soon he was guarding railroad construction crews against Indian attacks. They had several brushes with the Indians, and what impressed him most was the Indian's courage and ability to fight so hard with so little. The Indians with their war bonnets streaming behind them as they rode their pintos and spotted ponies in battle was a sight to stir an adventuresome youth. The danger and excitement were fully up to his expectations.

Dad wrote of the severe action at Turkey Creek, where they had a running fight with several hundred Indians. A bullet went through his hat brim. He looked at it seriously and said to his bunkie, "That will be handy when I hang it up!" Many were not so lucky; a number of his company were killed and others went to the tent hospital. Horses of killed Indians ran in confusion, and those poor beasts that had been wounded squealed and snorted as they tried to escape. Finally, through the dust cloud Dad saw a mass of Indians stringing out to the west. The fight was over. The company then took stock. During the process a mule got scared and ran a wagon wheel over Dad's foot. The doctor sent him to the hospital but he was out in a week. "You can't keep a good man down," was his comment.

Then men had little to do for a while and so they went hunting buffalo. They would cut off the hind quarters and put poison in the remaining part to get wolves and coyotes. They'd sell the pelts for seventy-five cents each, and this helped to supplement their pay. Privates like Dad got thirteen dollars a month. He estimated that they killed around a hundred buffalo before they left. He was getting so good, he said, he could shoot almost as well as he played billiards, which wasn't bad.

Dad was discharged on November 15, 1867, by reason of "Muster Out of Company." He had enlisted at Harper on July 15, 1867, his age at enrollment being nineteen. His discharge read: "Honorable discharge in campaigns against the Cheyennes, Kiowas, Arapahoes, and Comanches."

After his discharge he went to Ellsworth City, Kansas, a place famous for its straight-shooting marshal, gun fighters, Indian scouts, frontiersmen, and well-dressed card men, the latter being not too popular. He saw three gamblers chased out of town the first night he was there. He went to work in a combination pool-billiard hall and saloon, and wrote, "I never drank anything stronger than a glass of beer because drink dulls one's wits; but billiards, I took them all on whenever I could."

The day after he arrived they hung three rustlers in front of the livery barn. Nobody seemed to think anything of it. One day Dad met Wild Bill Hickok. He did not appear at all wild; in fact, he was an honest, open-hearted, very brave man. He could really use the guns.

Dad and Hickok played quite a few games, mostly poker, but when Dad suggested billiards Hickok just shook his head and winked. "I heard about you, John. You're too sharp, but you do it square and that's more than they do in poker games in the saloon, so I hear." However, in spite of his distaste for saloon poker, Hickok did sit down in one, and they must have *let* him win because he left the game with over a hundred dollars. They were taking no chances with guns that could talk. Hickok had a keen, alert look and moved quietly as a cat.

There was much freight moving up from the Mexican border, and lots of cattle were brought to Ellsworth to be shipped East. Ellsworth City was a supply point and terminal for freight outfits from the border and Army posts. One day about twenty-five wagons, drawn by eight or ten oxen each, pulled in from New Mexico. All the help were Mexicans, a fun-loving, jovial bunch, but at the same time rought and tough. That night a bartender friend of Dad by the name of Young tried to quell a too boisterous group. In the gun fight that followed a man was killed. The bartender was arresed and tried in the next room. An hour later he was freed, but he had to get out of town in a hurry because the Mexicans would have made short work of him if they could have laid hands on him.

A few days later another man was shot in the pool parlor. He crawled out into the night and they found him near the door—dead. Then another man was found in the back of the saloon with two bullets through his head. This was too much. The marshal made all the saloons close up until the whisky was absorbed and tension eased off a little; things were moving so fast anything could have happened.

An old Mexican wagon train man came to the saloon a number of times to play pool with Dad and they got pretty friendly, the Mexican being interesting to talk with. He told Dad he had a boy about Dad's age, and he sure tried to beat Dad at pool, but to no avail. Finally he said, "Americano too fast. I like Americano. You go with us, we have fun, yes?" When the wagon train pulled out for Fort Union, New Mexico, there was Dad up with the driver, but the more he thought of the situation the less he liked it. He had started to go West and here he was heading South!

Evidently he looked pretty down in the mouth, for the boss noticed his dejection and, thinking him lonesome or homesick, said, "You no like? I fix. I have three daughters. When we get there you pick." Dad told him women were fine but not in his plans. Just the same, the Mexican kept saying, "When we get to Albuquerque, you get Marie, Yvonne, or Jojo, you like."

The old Mexican spoke some English, mostly cuss words, and they got along fine. There was much to keep them busy. This was a wild new trail, long and dusty, and the Indians came and went. They had to circle the wagons every night and put out a watch. But all that happened was some thieving. After many weeks, they arrived at Fort Union, then on to Albuquerque where Dad left the train, chalking the enterprise up to experience, as he put it.

However, before they parted the old Mexican, true to his word, took Dad home with him where they had drinks and a nice big supper. The girls were much in evidence and the Mexican asked him, "Which one you want, Americano?" The dark, mischievous eyes of the girls danced and shone like stars at this, but Dad was not in the marrying mood. He just gave them a big smile and said he would have to move on. But he was touched, for when a Mexican takes someone into his patio it means he really likes him.

Dad still wanted to see the Old West, the Indian country, and the buffalo range. He wanted to hunt for gold (the lure of gold is strange—and dangerous at times!), and prove he wasn't a weakling as some seemed to think. He joined another wagon train headed for Fort Windgate, New Mexico, not far from the Arizona border. This was a prospecting and mining party, but not a successful one. A quarrel broke out when they reached Fort Windgate, the group fell apart, and Dad was left stranded and broke.

Disgusted but not discouraged, he enlisted in the 37th U.S.

Infantry on August 29, 1868, for three years. Soon he was transferred to Company C, 3d U.S. Infantry, and he served until August 3, 1870, when, to his surprise, he was suddenly honorably discharged by special order. His parents had caught up with him! So he ended up going back to Connecticut and into his father's business.

His father was prosperous and wanted to "save" his son from the West and the Indians, so he made every inducement to hold Dad. His salary jumped from $15 to $150 a month, and Dad stayed put. His friends wanted to hear his stories of the West but, oddly enough, at that time he did not like to talk of his Western experiences.

On May 17, 1872, after a beautiful courtship, he married Philene Abigail Eunice Parker. It was a happy marriage and three girls were born, Clara, Ethel, and Marie, all very beautiful, according to Dad. But on October 13, 1881, tragedy struck; their mother died, and Dad had to get a housekeeper. As the years went by and the girls grew older, there were other housekeepers, for Dad never remarried. But he was growing increasingly restless. All this time he had subdued his desire to go West and to search for gold. Gold, that siren of the prospector! "Easy gold," as they say, and lots of it. Faraway places and adventures had a terrific fascination for Dad, and finally he could resist no longer. The girls had grown into womanhood, with Clara and Marie married, and Ethel able to take care of herself, for she had gotten a job with the telephone company.

One day it happened! Headlines in the papers in 1898: GOLD IN KLONDIKE, GOLD ON THE BEACH AT NOME, GOLD! GOLD! GOLD! Dad said, "I can't help it, girls, it sure does stir something in me!" He held off two years, then in April 1900 the time had come. He went to Alaska, not by wagon train this time, but by the Great Northern Railroad to Seattle, then by boat to the "promised land." He wrote: "The train was loaded to capacity with gold-seekers, all hopeful and bound for Alaska; old men, young men, and women, all talking gold and most knowing little about it, but all gold-crazy and all rarin' to go."

Here is an excerpt from another letter: "I found sleeping quarters hard to get, equipment hard to get; excitement, action, and congestion everywhere. Passage to Alaska was hard to get."

He complained too about not hearing from the girls. They were writing to him faithfully, but I guess he must have been moving too often for mail to catch up with him.

Again he wrote: "After many weeks I got a very good outfit together, and some chance friends and I got passage on an English boat hauling coal for China. Hungry for money, they loaded the vessel with all the gold-crazy men and women they could get. We had scant sleeping space, barely enough food for the trip, and few medical supplies. There was no heat, the weather was bad, the food poor, the people irritable. Several men died and were buried at sea. Finally, after twenty-one days of misery and suffering, we sighted Nome, Alaska. It was beautiful, but we were in no mood for beauty.

"Everything here has a newness about it, log cabins with dirt roofs and board shacks all covered with snow. This is the first feeling of loneliness I have had. It is such a terrible feeling that I must down it and buck up and win. The ice is so heavy and thick that we cannot dock the boat, green water and bluish-green ice tapering off to turquoise, then white and all shades of the rainbow, beautiful and dangerous. Many of the men and women have left the boat and are plodding slowly over the ice for shore. They are so glad to get off this old boat, this coal ship where we have been so miserable, that any change is welcome; besides, they want that 'easy gold' and quick. Some are strong, resourceful, and capable. Others expected the gold to be lying here on top of the ground to be picked up. But Nature guards her gold jealously and in effect says, 'None but the brave and strong deserve my gold.' The reaction of a few, only a very few I am glad to say, has been pitiful; they just look petrified when faced with reality.

"I fully believe I can do anything any other man can do. If gold is here I will try, try, and try again. Besides, on the boat four men and myself arranged a partnership, each putting in one thousand dollars. The partnership was started in Seattle between two of us, then we took in two more on the boat, so now we are four. One is an experienced prospector and miner. No names are mentioned since names do not count for much up here anyway; it is just what you are that counts in a place like this."

A few days later this letter came: "Dear Ethel, we got our equipment and supplies ashore. Have set up a temporary camp and left a man to guard our outfit. Food must be guarded with one's very life since so many do not have enough food. How they expect to live I do not see. Large men who can pack a good load are in demand. I heard one big Swede boasting in a beer hall, 'I yust so strong like mule; gold, I get him plenty, five hundred dollars yesterday and more tomorrow.' I believe him. I saw him down about twenty whiskies without a chaser, and he didn't blink an eye. I and many of the other miners have loads to carry, so men like him are really in demand, and they get their price.

"The three of us prospected all day Thursday and part of Friday before we discovered any colors that amounted to much. Tonight I am thinking of you. No letters! Do write to me, my dear girls, even if you get no answer, as I may be a long way from a post office, and you get no answer, and the boats do not leave regularly. The last boat leaves soon and it will be a long time until spring, so I hope to get your letters before the ice closes in. But write anyway. Goodbye. Love, Dad."

In a later letter he wrote: "The beach at Nome in 1900 is like a beehive, people everywhere, and all gold-crazy, so we had quite a time locating! We have one of the best outfits— three tents, a boiler, pans, a gold rocker, a little lumber, and some canvas, along with provisions for six months. Tonight we are quite happy. Four tired men have over one hundred dollars in gold dust and a few nuggets. I am going to save a big one for little Ethel in far-away Connecticut. Hope I get a dandy!

"One night the 'experienced' miner said, 'Boys, we ought to

move and quick. I got a dandy place located. Old Slim Smith is up there and he said he got five thousand dollars last week. It must be true, for he's spending mighty freely.'

"I was for staying where we were, but there were three against me, so it was pull stakes and move about three miles. We camped closer to the sea and lower down. We did not have much protection from the sea lashing down from the north. We did not do so well. Some days we got gold, but it was mostly fine stuff and hard to save. At times we would get about an ounce, at other times a trace and a few small, smooth nuggets, which indicated that we were farther from the source here than at the other location. I suggested that we return to the old claim, but found that we hardly had moved our stuff out when another bunch moved in.

"I heard they were doing pretty good but one hears so much here that there is little you can believe. If they are getting a lot of gold, that is when they don't say anything, but as a matter of fact, I heard later that we really had a bonanza and gave it up on the fool notion of that experienced (?) miner. Our successors took out six thousand dollars a week for three weeks. Later I heard the total take was forty-five thousand dollars. We did not get along so well from then on, and finally we bought out our 'experienced' miner for fifty dollars.

"We began to do a little better when we moved our rocker higher up, but it was still nip and tuck all summer. The nights were getting frosty in early September. Our outfit held council. We decided we would move our gear into Nome City, store it, and hole up until spring. We would stick together and try some other place then. We thought we had learned a lot now and we had confidence in one another. Good partners are hard to get, especially in a new gold-diggings.

"It was early fall in 1900 and we knew the winters were long up in the land of the Midnight Sun, so three tired and somewhat discouraged men retired tonight, each to his own sleeping bag. I had the gold pouch which contained about forty ounces of gold dust, forty ounces representing the hardest, most grueling work I had ever done. I am tough as a pine knot now. Late in the night I noticed the wind flapping the tent a lot, but I like the sound of the wind and the waves, so I went off to sleep again. Then I sort of slipped off the cot onto the sand. I put out my hand and felt water, several inches of it. It was sea water coming in in little waves, but they were getting bigger. I quickly woke my pals, saying, 'Fellows, we got to get out of here quick, the sea is coming in.' They looked puzzled. So little happens here that they wondered what. I repeated, 'Men, it's flood water or something. We got to get out!'

"They got into their clothes in a hurry, and a good thing too, for suddenly the wind screamed like a siren and the tent started to jump. As I went out of the tent, I heard a guy-rope snap. The end whipped across my face so hard it made the blood come. Then that tent and the other tents just seemed to soar straight up and disappear, and the three of us were standing in the open. At that moment a big wave came in and knocked my pals over. It was almost too dark to see. Another wave nearly upset me, but I made a dive for where my bunk had been to save our mutual gold poke. I could not locate it. What a chill I felt! Was all that work for nothing? I heard the fellows yell, 'Get out of there, man!' Then a big wave knocked me down as it passed, and I decided like the others that I had best hit for high ground. The roar of the waves was terrific and the howl of the wind increased the din. I could hear others shout, so I knew we were not the only ones in trouble.

"We ran as fast as we could, but those waves, one after another, would bowl us over like pins in a bowling alley. At last, after what seemed an interminable time of fighting waves and bucking the wind, we reached high ground. Then a cold, freezing rain began to pelt down on us, but we kept traveling until we found a brushy spot that broke the wind a little. There we stayed until the first streak of dawn. Dark clouds scudded across the sky. As it got lighter, we saw other groups, but on the beach, there were only ruins and breakers. Everything was lost, that was easy to see! I wondered how many had lost their lives. I could see heavy boilers and equipment being heaved about and blown out to sea. There was all kinds of debris headed seaward. The water was sweeping far up on the beach and beyond that all was wreckage and desolation. It was a sad sight, and worse still, all our work was lost!

"We trudged into Nome, got dried out, and had some hot food.

"It sure hit the spot and cheered us a little, and we learned just how badly the storm had dealt with the prospectors. Thousands of them, including ourselves, had lost everything. It was an unusually severe one for so early in the season, but some old sourdough said they had seen worse. However, the beach had not been occupied by thousands then as it was this time.

"I had less than five hundred dollars on me of my own money. So now what to do? The storm finally died down somewhat and we went back to look for the gold. We couldn't even locate the spot where our camp had been; wind and waves can cause terrible damage. We returned to Nome City, a dejected, discouraged lot. Easy gold—where was it? 'What fools we mortals be!' I feel badly because I lost your nuggets, Ethel, as well as the dust. I must get more."

After some pondering, Dad and his partners, along with many others, decided to take the next boat for Seattle, where they arrived safely after a long, stormy trip. He now had only $390 left. As he later said, "I couldn't go back to my friends and my girls broke. I said to myself, 'Oh well, you're only a little over fifty. The West has many chances for a good man!' "

He got a job with a jewelry repair shop and did quite well until spring. One day he met a friend from Alaska and the gold fever began to stir again. They decided to go to Ketchikan late in 1902. Ketchikan was only an outpost of civilization at this time, merely a trading and fishing post. Supplies were sledded in by dog-team. The partner did not tarry long. He went on to other diggings, but Dad stayed. He wrote to the girls, telling them of his whereabouts and saying, "I keep writing to you girls but no answers come. Perhaps I don't deserve answers. I am pretty much of a failure, I fear."

Ethel recalled the last letter she got from her father was from Ketchikan in 1907. When no further word came, she finally wrote to the postmaster. He replied that her father had been there but was gone now and that he had no forwarding address. So the trail ended.

We decided to search as best as we could. We put a notice in the paper and got a letter from Colorado from a man who said he knew John Pomeroy, and knew he was alive. We answered the letter and wrote several times, but no reply ever came.

Ethel and I moved from Great Falls, Montana, to Post Falls, Idaho, where I worked in the woods and on ranches. When our son John was born, we named him after her father. Four years passed; we were still seeking a clew to John Pomeroy's whereabouts. In 1919 we moved to Spokane. We still believed Dad to be alive. We moved into our own house in Spokane. Ethel's sister Clara died in Arkansas. We moved again, to a little tract of land just west of Spokane. All this time we kept tracing every clew, but always came to a dead end, always.

One day a show came to the Orpheum in Spokane, "The Days of 1898," an Alaskan story. It was advertised that anyone who had had relatives in the gold rush would get a free ticket. Of course we went, and there was a little story in the paper about it and about our search for John Pomeroy. In about a week, we received a letter from a man in the "big house" in Nevada, very poorly written, saying he had seen the article in the paper, that he had known a man answering to John Pomeroy's description in Goldfield, but that the man had left Goldfield and gone, he thought, to Sacramento. Again we sent out letters, and finally wrote to the postmaster in Sacramento who replied that there was no such person there.

After several moves, we finally in 1932 settled in Spokane, buying the house in which I still live. Poor Ethel often spoke of her dad, but we agreed that he probably was dead by now.

We struggled on and put our youngsters through school. Then came Ethel's stroke and, after four years of invalidism, her death in 1943. I thought, "Well, perhaps since we couldn't find her dad on earth, they are reunited now."

A year after her passing I returned home from work one evening, reached into the mailbox, and pulled out a letter addressed to Ethel. It was from the Skip Tracer Co. of New York. I had a queer feeling as I looked at the envelope. Could it possibly be they found the old man after all these years? What a tragedy! She gone, he perhaps still here!

I opened the letter. Here it is, word for word, dated November 17, 1944.

Dear Madam:

We are seeking the whereabouts of Ethel, Camelia, Clara Agnes, and Marie Elmira, daughters of John and Abigail Pomeroy. The mother of these girls died in Connecticut about 1885, and he was last heard from at the turn of the century. After a lengthy search, we have reason to believe you are one of the aforementioned. We will appreciate any information you may give us. We may have some very interesting news for your branch of the Pomeroy family.

Needless to say, I answered immediately and gave them all the data I had. I was an old man now and had seen a lot. I do not cry easily, but this brought tears to my eyes. I thought, what strange things life does to people. Why do people delay, postpone, or forget to write to relatives and friends? Contacts are always important and doubly so as one grows older and has time to think.

I soon received a reply to my letter, saying that J. H. Pomeroy was alive and well and financially able to take care of himself, but that he was desirous of hearing from his daughters and grandchildren. He was now ninety-nine, had fallen on a slippery street in San Francisco and broken his hip, and was in the Veterans Hospital at Napa, California, having been admitted as a veteran of the Indian Wars. (Our family Bible says he was two years older, but when one is touching the century mark a year or so more or less is immaterial. Records were not too good then anyway.

Immediately my daughter Florence and son Bob and I went to California to see the old gentleman. How happy he was that he had found us! He was the pet of the hospital. They called him the "old man" and they appreciated his stories of the old buffalo and Indian days and the gold rush. The Veterans Hospital at Napa is a very fine institution and he was getting the best of care. One of the girls he had left so long ago was still alive—Marie, the youngest—and she too hastened to California to see her father, and she stayed with him until his death from cancer in 1946. What a happy man he was to have found his remaining daughter and five grandchildren!

It was Captain Merrit of the hospital who had become interested and gotten the New York company to try and find Dad's family. Captain Merrit said he would see Dad sitting quietly with tears in his eyes, though when anyone approached he would wipe the tears away and look unconcerned. One day Captain Merrit asked, "John, what is troubling you?"

Dad answered, "Oh, I guess I am just an old fool; most of us get that way once in a while. But I sure would like to find my little girls."

Captain Merrit did the rest.

Captain Merrit said this about John H. Pomeroy: "Tall, well dressed, well liked by all who knew him. He carried his age remarkably well and few could realize he was so old. As late as 1942, when past ninety-five, he was still an expert shot at pool and billiards. His fine sense of humor and alert mind kept him as modern in thought and action as a person fifty years younger.

"It was January 1953 that he slipped on the wet pavement, injuring his hip, and was sent to the Veterans Hospital at Napa as a veteran of the Indian Wars. He has been here ever since. During the years he spent with us, he always took daily walks through the grounds when the weather permitted. He was a constant reader of Western stories, newspapers, and magazines. He keeps abreast of the times and all events as avidly as a much younger person. He had a host of friends because he was so lovable. He was a member of the General Custer Camp of Indian War Veterans of San Francisco."

What had happened to John during those "lost" years? I had better let him tell the story the way he related it to me when I asked him why he stopped writing:

"That's a big question and I can hardly answer it. I did write for a time but the letters evidently didn't get through and I became discouraged. It got so it seemed I couldn't write and if I didn't write I didn't deserve letters, did I? Also, I kept thinking of those nuggets I had promised. I must make good on them, I thought, then I would return. The years passed. I hardly realized how old I was getting. Then one day I stopped and thought. I was appalled at how the time had gone by.

"Did I get lonely? Of course there were times when I was very lonely and felt I was a failure, but I held to the hope of making good and returning to my beloved girls a big success. When I was in Ketchikan, the mail didn't come in often and then only by dog team over long and snow-covered trails that were rough and dangerous. I remained in Alaska until 1907.

"About this time there were stories of big gold strikes in Nevada which interested me, and I asked myself, should I go? I had a few thousand now, perhaps I could win. I returned to the States and went to Goldfield, Nevada, where I entered a partnership deal that did not pan out as I thought it should. I sold out. Immediately the deal paid off big to the others. Lady Luck was giving me the brush off.

"I moved from place to place with no permanent address, often thinking of my little girls and wondering how they were now. Shucks, guess they have forgotten me anyway, I thought, for I am just an old failure. I now went to Reno where I took over a pool hall on a fifty-fifty basis. I did pretty well there, better than in the gold diggings. I now had pool, billiards, card tables, and a saloon. I bought mining stock right and left, for I was determined to go back to my girls with gold, or not to go back at all. I wrote to the girls but my letters came back. I wondered why they didn't write to me. The years were passing and I was getting older.

"In 1909 I sold out in Reno and put a lot of money in mining stock. I played billiards and won a lot; I just played the gentleman for a while and did little else. My mining stock was not going up. In fact, it proved of little value. One day I heard Tex Rickard needed a good gunman at the Jeffries-Johnson fight to be held in Reno on July 10, 1910. I got the job and they put me in the forty-dollar section, gave me a gun and a powerful water hose. I had orders to use my own judgment as to when, or if, to use either of the weapons. Several times I was afraid I might have to pacify some of the boys, but, thank goodness, the pressure did not quite reach the boiling point. I was glad when the fight ended, even though a little excitement now and then is good for the heart. I knew I could hit the mark with a gun, but wasn't so sure about the hose. But what a fight! It was pitiful to see the poor condition Jim Jeffries was in, and the terrible beating he took from Johnson.

"The fight fans were a wild bunch that night. I often wondered what would have happened if someone had hit one of those colored boys in the eye, for, believe me, they were pretty overbearing and insulting. If looks could have killed, there would have been a lot of casualties! Race feelings ran high and lots of fans didn't want to see a Negro win at any price. But fight fans as a rule are real sportsmen and like fair play, so it all came off pretty clean.

"Now the adventure call was coming more and more strongly. As I said before, my mining stock was not proving profitable. Still I continued to buy. It might be a fool's game but I felt that by the simple law of averages I might win something. I didn't like roulette or cards, for I had seen too much of these games close up. Finally in 1911 I decided to leave Reno. I stopped and worked a short time in Sacramento. Then I went on to San Francisco where I worked in a hotel as night clerk for several months.

"The gold bug kept biting and I joined up with two other miners. We bought supplies and equipment and went to 'Shirt Tail' Canyon, about twelve miles from Colfax, California. We did quite well for a while, and when it began to taper off we sold out and separated. Those were the days of big strikes and I had my sights set high. I thought that surely I too would hit it big sometimes and be able to take that nugget home to little Ethel as I had promised.

"I now went to Iowa Hill, California, for a time; then I went back to Colfax where I had many friends and, I thought, a better chance. I bought several pool and billiard tables, some gambling equipment, and a bar in Nevada City and had the equipment trucked to Colfax. Soon I was doing quite well. I bought some property and more mining stock. I also had occasion in my business to stake old miners and prospectors. Sometimes I wondered if they didn't have me pegged for an easy mark—so few could or did pay back the advances. However, I like to believe they all tried even though that part of my business was pretty much of a washout.

"Most Westerners, particularly the gambling type, are generous to a fault. They'd rather help a little than see misery and starvation. The old fellows digging for gold asked for so little.

"One day I was on a business trip to Reno and went into an establishment. Quite a crowd was gathered around a roulette wheel. The center of interest was a man I had known while in Alaska. He was using twenty-dollar gold pieces for chips and he was winning, too. I nodded to him and said, 'See you're busy, Jack.'

"He waved jovially and replied, 'Sure am, an' havin' fun too. Stick aroun', pard, we'll buy drinks later. Four yellow boys on twenty-nine an' two on the black.'

"The croupier spun the little wheel, and sure enough it was twenty-nine on the black. I stood there and saw him win twenty-eight thousand dollars. I kept on standing and watched him begin to lose. At last, his winnings gone, he quit, the loser by two thousand dollars. But he was a good loser and said to me. 'Put her there, old pard, we'll have that drink now!' Truly, Lady Luck is a fickle one! I tried to get him interested in staying here with me. But he said, 'No, no, that stuff's not for me; I'm for the North when the ice goes out. There's gold up there!'

"I returned to my business, but soon sold out and bought more mining stock. In 1920 I began receiving a small government pension for my services in the Indian Wars. With that and what I received from my property, I decided to go to San Francisco and take it easy, and for about seventeen years I lived at the Lankersham Hotel on Fifth near Market Street. I had many friends and played a lot of billiards. My greatest vice, if vice it can be called, was smoking good cigars. I always liked a good cigar and the company of a beautiful woman, though I was never what you would call a real lady's man. My first and only true love was Abigail Parker, the mother of my children and a real pal.

"Even so, I got along pretty well with the ladies, for I always tried to be a gentleman. I like to look at pretty women and I admire their technique in beautifying themselves. God was very good to man when he made women so interesting and beautiful; I mean good women. Believe me, I've seen lots of the other kind both here and in Alaska, and a lot of them I really pitied. Yes, give me a good cigar and a nice lady and the others can take the drink.

"I think the greatest days of my life were the years I spent in San Francisco: the daily walks, the daily game of billiards, often with prominent people, and the visits with friends—all helped to keep my health and spirits at par."

I asked him one day what was the most humorous incident he could remember of his days in the Old West.

He laughingly replied, "That would be hard to say, there were so many of them. But I always get a laugh when I think of this one: You remember my telling you about Wild Bill Hickok? Well, I got to know him pretty well. When I was about nineteen I was employed in a railroad eating house at Salinas, Kansas. Things were new and rough. I was in the kitchen when I heard quite a commotion in the dining room. Someone was rapping on the table and talking very loud. Suddenly the landlady rushed in. Mrs. Babersnite, from New York. She started berating the man for being so noisy. She had a pretty vitriolic tongue and a complete vocabulary of profanity. She was something of a holy terror.

"Anyway, she tied into this noisy customer in a big way. I peepd through the door and recognized my old friend Wild Bill Hickok. I expected to see some sparks fly. I wondered how he would handle a redheaded woman. She was telling him off pretty loud and some of the names she was using were right fancy. There was a tense stillness in the room. Some of the customers were looking pretty uneasy, and they had a right to be uneasy.

"Bill listened, then he gave her a long look and said, 'Lady, just thank your lucky stars you're not a man. Now bring on that food an' do it damned quick!' He came down with his fist on the table with a bang and the sugar bowl jumped up and spilled onto a chair. I guess she discovered they were two of a kind, for she wheeled around, trotted to the kitchen, and sent his order in, and all returned to peace and quiet on the dining front."

I asked him for the most exciting incident of his travels. He replied, "You want the most exciting incident? That's too difficult. There were so many. For instance, I had a pretty tense moment or two up in Ketchikan in 1906. I had been turnkey for the jail there and knew all about the people thereabouts. One day I was called to serve on the jury. They were trying a man for murder. Justice up there was pretty swift at times and sometimes pretty crude—not that killing was always considered a crime. Sometimes there were men who just asked for it; other times a trial was used to get rid of someone. On this particular occasion, I was convinced the man was inno-cent, so I decided to get him off. The only way seemed to be to hang the jury. Remember, this was not here in the States. At first I was alone, but gradually I won one after another of the jurors over to my way of thinking. We stuck it out until they had to turn the man loose. If looks ever killed any-body, some of us on that jury would have been laid away!"

John H. Pomeroy died in 1946 at the hospital and received a veteran's burial there. He had arrived at the hospital the year his daughter died in Spokane, still searching for her dad.

What strange things life does to us! How could a man write such beautiful, descriptive letters to the little girls he loved so deeply, and then years later say, "I just can't write any more"? So many things in life are past understanding.

I finish the story of John H. Pomeroy with this thought:

> *Live for those who love you,*
> *For those whose hearts are true,*
> *For the heaven that smiles above you,*
> *And the good that you may do.*
>   —UNKNOWN

I BEGIN TO PAINT

I was in the kitchen cooking my lonely breakfast one morning when I said aloud, "Now what to do? How can I live like this?"

Something seemed to say, "Why don't you paint? You've always wanted to."

I sighed and shook my head. It's too late, I thought. Why, I'm sixty-four! I seemed to hear, "Try it! Try it and see what happens!"

The idea stuck and I couldn't get rid of it. I finally did begin to paint again, and some people really liked my pictures of the Old West. I sold quite a few paintings.

I got a job with the Spokane Park Department and worked there for a couple of summers, painting in the winter months. I worked in a restaurant for a couple of rush seasons, painting every minute I got off the job.

I began wondering about Olive Scott, thinking of her marriage and wondering how it had turned out. It hit me with kind of a shock when I realized how long it had been since I'd seen or heard from her. I wondered if life had done as much to Ollie as it did to me. Well, I could find out, couldn't I?

I went to visit relatives in Great Falls. What changes the years had made! What had been a small village was now a fine, thriving city. The little elm trees planted so many years ago were now great trees that spread their branches high over the wide streets. There were modern business buildings, big stores, and paved roads. The district we used to call the sand hills was now covered with trim houses, and towering over all this scene stood a smokestack 506 feet high, like a guardian angel protecting the pygmies running hither and yon at its feet.

Livery barns had been replaced by gas stations with their red pumps and cokes on ice. Gone too were the prairie trails; all were fenced and plowed under, as in Charley Russell's picture, "Trails Plowed Under." Gone were the great buffalo herds, the old-time punchers who lived such carefree lives. Everything was changed. Whether I liked it or not, there it was. Changed.

I thought back to the time Charley Russell and I were putting our horses in the livery barn in Great Falls. A couple of men with him had had a few drinks too many. I guess it was "fighting whisky" they'd had, because they were in a fighting mood.

Charley said, "Come on, you bozos, you look like hell shot full of holes; let's go to the Mint—the drinks are on me."

Charley was quite a pacifier. He often poured water on the flames of anger.

I was leading a little Indian cayuse I sometimes rode, a mouse-colored, funny-looking animal with black-tipped ears. He was tough and I could travel far on him. Charley gave my horse a queer look. "What you got there, kid? Some kind of goat?"

I was just a kid and I didn't like the idea of anybody making fun of my horse. I told him very belligerently, "Well anyhow, your horse don't look so good spotted like an old cow."

Charley laughed and slapped me on the back. "That's right, kid, stick up for your horse. Sometimes a horse is a fellow's best friend."

I remembered how Charley used to night-herd horses. He knew horses and loved them. I think that's why he painted so many pictures of horses. He sure was the world's best painter of Western scenes, and all of us old punchers love what he put on canvas.

I visited at Ben Stevens' place. Ben was married to my niece Gladys Blaine, and rented part of my father's old place, the old Stork Ranch that had been carved out of the wilderness so long ago. It was good to be back, taking a look around.

A few days later I went over to the old Scott place where Ollie had lived. Her brother Gerald was running the farm and doing very well. I cautiously inquired about Ollie. He told me, "Oh, Ollie's working in the diet kitchen at Bremerton, getting along just fine. She's raised three children an' is a widow now."

This was all I wanted to know. Ollie a widow? Well, now maybe I was being a darned fool, getting romantic at my age.

I returned to Ben's place and he suggested taking me up to Old Tiger Butte where I had lived forty-six years ago. I was glad to go, and soon we were riding in his car and I was thinking it was a pretty good world after all. We crossed Sand Coulee Creek and were going upgrade toward the bench land on the east side when I happened to look behind us. I saw a cloud of boiling smoke rising back near Eden that sure looked dangerous.

We turned around and made it fast down the hill. We could already see the fire burning near Centerville around the hills clear to the edge of Ming Coulee. Apparently it had been started by someone looking for excitement. It would be just too bad for anybody who did something like that if they got caught. Ben and I finally were in the thickest of the smoke along with the neighborhood farmers, all of us fighting the flames that were burning up good grass and fences. We fought with wet sacks, water carried in buckets, in tubs; in fact, we carried water in anything handy. I knew what prairie fires could do, the horror of them, for I had battled them in years gone by.

The worst calamities always end sometime, and so it was with this one. Several farmers, including Ben Stevens, had to move their cattle out to other districts to get pasture, and one man with a bad heart died fighting the flames. We did save most of the buildings, and that helped.

A few days after this excitement, I returned to Spokane. I wrote a long letter to Ollie, the girl of my boyhood dreams. She answered promptly with a newsy letter, and for a while we carried on a nice correspondence.

Then Ollie came to Spokane as a delegate to a meeting of the Children's Benefit Society, and we had a good visit. Just before she returned, I asked her a question. She answered me, "Not now, it will have to be later." I'll tell you, my hopes rose. She hadn't exactly said no. I felt happier than I had for some time.

It wasn't many weeks till Ollie had her vacation. She dropped me a card, saying she was going to Wyoming to visit relatives and would stop over on the way to see me. I met the dear little lady and showed her a good time in Spokane, after which she went on to Wyoming as she had planned.

After a couple of weeks I received a letter, saying, "I am returning now. Please meet me at the bus terminal." Needless to say, I was eagerly waiting when the bus pulled in.

I took her out to lunch. We were sitting at a little table for two when I asked her what time she was taking the bus for Bremerton. She gave me the sweetest smile and said, blushing, "Why, I'm not going back this time—unless you say so!"

I didn't say so, and on November 23, 1947, we were married. After forty-six years Ollie was mine!

Everyone was wonderful to us. Ollie's children and my own tried to outdo one another with their attentions to us. They gave us three wedding dinners, a three-story wedding cake, lots of presents, and special attention at the wedding dance. There were stories about us and pictures of our wedding in the Montana and Washington newspapers. One reporter had to have his little joke; he wrote: "Stork had to wait forty-six years for the competition to thin out before he got his girl."

Maybe I did have to wait a long time to claim my girl, but the waiting was worth it, for we are very happy together.

That reporter was more right than he realized, though, for in those old days in Montana girls were few, there was plenty of competition, many amusing incidents, as well as a few fist fights. Anything was fair in love then, as always, and Lillie and Ollie Scott, two beautiful girls, had their full share of attention from the young men for miles around. Both girls were accomplished, they played the organ well, they could sing like birds, they were graceful dancers, and they sure looked good on horses.

Ollie and I love now to talk about the days of the Old West in the "Land of the Shining Mountains"; we think we could never have chosen a better time or place to grow up. My Ollie! My true-blue companion, my wonderful cook and house-keeper. What peace we enjoy!

CONCLUSION

THESE stories of the Old West are all true, except that in a few instances names have been changed. My aim in writing them has been to try to convey the feelings and spirit of the people mentioned, to give their reactions to the hardships they encountered in the conquering of the Old West.

I have tried to point out to this generation that the frontiersman had much to do besides rustle cattle and shoot it out, as the Wild West stories written in New York skyscrapers and Hollywood studios would have people believe.

Of course some of the Hollywood riders can do stunts on horseback that no cowboy with all his senses would think of trying. We never tried to make our horse buck—believe me, they didn't need any coaxing on a cold morning out there by the rope corral on the prairie.

But it is impossible to put across in words what we old cowpunchers knew and what is missing in present-day living. It was great to be free in a land where gates and fences were few and life made demands on both mind and body.

You who live in our great country, keep it great, good, beautiful, and as free as possible, for there are still frontiers. My emphasis on the old frontiers does not mean that I discount the new ones. There will always be new frontiers. People may, one of these days, be traveling to and from the moon and Mars. There may be a smart bunch up on those planets. They may know a lot more than we do here on earth. Yet even here on earth there are still large areas unexplored and undeveloped. Yes, there will be new frontiers, maybe just as exciting as those I knew—and there are still the frontiers of science, philosophy, art, and medicine to conquer.

But Ollie and I have memories of days that people in these speedy times will never know; and, not knowing, perhaps never miss. Who knows? Anyway, that's the way life is.

Yours sincerely,

RAWHIDE SHORTY